TENNIS AND THE MASAI

When he got back to his room, Martin locked the door in case Mrs Fist should feel like a smoke and sat down to write to his parents. He had not written since his postcard from Nairobi. He told them everything that had happened to him at Haggard Hall. Smith-Baggot, the rhino droppings, how he had carried a rifle and led a wild tribesman through the jungle. He mentioned the leopard in passing and hinted that he might have to do something about it in the morning. *'The head-master says that if we find the pi-dog we can dose it with strychnine,'* he wrote. *'Leopards always return to their kill, and that's the way to get them. It happens a lot out here.'*

Out here. He wondered how his letter would go down in Purley Way. Probably his mother would read it to Gran and then to Mrs Simmonds at number fourteen. Martin sealed the envelope and switched off the light. Somehow Purley Way and all its works suddenly seemed very far away.

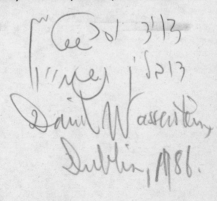

David Wasserstein

Dublin, 1986.

TENNIS AND THE MASAI

Nicholas Best

ARROW BOOKS

Arrow Books Limited
62–65 Chandos Place, London WC2N 4NW

An imprint of Century Hutchinson Limited

London Melbourne Sydney Auckland Johannesburg
and agencies throughout the world

First published by Hutchinson 1986

Arrow edition 1987

© Nicholas Best 1986

Printed and bound in Great Britain by Anchor Brendon
Limited, Tiptree, Essex

ISBN 0 09 950370 0

She said, 'You'll like Kenya. It's always like this.'
Evelyn Waugh
Remote People.

The shape of the mountain, which was undoubtedly of volcanic origin, was almost round. . . . 'Behold the House of "*She-who-must-be-obeyed*!" ' he said. 'Had ever a queen such a throne before?'
H. Rider Haggard
She.

PART ONE

Tennis

1

On the narrow beach below Fort Jesus, a group of Germans were having a party. It was getting towards evening, and after the heat of the day they were glad to throw off their protective clothing at last and frolic naked in the shallows. From the Indian Ocean a late breeze had arisen, ruffling the flag of the republic of Kenya which had basked unassumingly above the battlements for most of the afternoon. The Germans danced in the breeze and bellowed with delight. They were tourists, uncircumcised mostly, enjoying the simple noisy pleasures of their kind. They splashed and sang, the men displaying tight Aryan muscles or an enormous beer belly according to age, the women exuberant white buttocks or the mottled abominations of the Munich hausfrau.

From the veranda of the Mombasa Club, sheltered behind palm trees, two officials of the administration sat side by side in identical cane chairs, observing the revellers on the beach. It was the hour of day at which, in colonial times, tea had been served, and the tradition had been scrupulously preserved. There was a cup of tea beside Mr District Commissioner Karanja, although shortly he would follow it up with the first whisky and soda of the evening; another at the elbow of Mr bin Seyd, superintendent of police.

'Look at them,' said bin Seyd. 'Look at the way they dance. I wonder if we ought to allow it.'

'There's no law against dancing. It would be impossible to enforce.'

'There's a law against nudity.' Mr bin Seyd was a devout coast Muslim. 'They've no right to strip off like that. It's illegal in a public place.'

One of the younger Germans had a tennis ball, which he had been bouncing up and down with ruthless Teutonic efficiency. He retrieved it now from the grassy stretch in front of the club. He was wearing a string of beads, purchased that morning in the bazaar, and nothing else. As he ran to collect the ball, it was difficult not to admire the pristine simplicity of his nakedness, the unaffected, savage good humour of his laugh. In common with the others on the beach, he had smeared his body all over with grease kept in a plastic bottle for the purpose. The result, in the evening sunlight, was a magnificent sheen.

'A pastoral people, in their way,' observed Karanja. 'One can't expect to change them overnight. They're tourists, after all. One doesn't want to frighten them off.'

'Nonetheless, Commissioner, it isn't right. You're the Bwana DC. You ought to do something.'

Karanja's was a life full of burden. 'There are times, you know, when I envy them their simplicity,' he confessed. 'Look at the way they're enjoying themselves. No cares, no worries. Happy as the day is long.'

He was beginning to tire of the Germans. He flicked his fly whisk irritably, and bin Seyd saw that the subject was closed. One after the other the two officials settled deeper into their chairs, the same chairs – or rather the same positions on the veranda – occupied by successive District Commissioners and superintendents of police for almost a hundred years. At the back of the veranda there were the same month-old copies of *Punch* and *Country Life* in leather folders; in front of it the same flagpole and bronze ship's cannon facing out to sea. The coast of East Africa has known many conquerors over the centuries – Turks, Arabs, Portuguese – and all have left their marks in various ways. But it had taken the English to build a club.

The first conquerors to leave a mark of any permanence were the Portuguese. On a coral ridge overlooking the old harbour they raised the bastion of Fort Jesus – Matodi in Evelyn Waugh's *Black Mischief* – nearly four hundred years ago, and for a century thereafter held it against Arab fleets from Oman. Sieges and shipwrecks were commonplace in the early days, sails from Lisbon a rarity. Plague, treachery and murder ruled the garrison. Men slipped over the wall at night, lowered on ropes, while their enemies waited in silence to behead them; others were assassinated, or blew themselves up in the powder magazine in their hour of defeat. Not until the coming of the British had the fort been able to relax. The walls since then had faded to a Mediterranean combination of tan, pink and blue, with bougainvillea along the ramparts and bushes of frangipani. The fort no longer served its original purpose but was simply a tourist attraction, the only building of any antiquity along the coast.

On the beach below, the Germans had found a tom-tom. It seemed unlikely that they would allow such a discovery to pass unnoticed. Nor did they.

'Happy as the day is long,' repeated Karanja above the din. 'How I envy them.'

Unlike bin Seyd, Karanja was a Kikuyu from up-country. For eight years, give or take a few months, he had been Commissioner in Mombasa, responsible for the administration of government among the alien, hostile people of the coast. Religious and tribal differences separated him from the population under his control, a cultural gap impossible to span. He was a lonely man. He spent his days sitting in judgment, giving out the law, presiding over a thousand trivial disputes, a thousand familiar accusations of corruption and incompetence. His wife, Kikuyu like himself, complained repeatedly of the heat at sea level. They looked forward to the day when they could retire to the house they had bought in the heart of the Kenya highlands. Karanja hesitated to call it a cottage. Often, as an apprentice administrator, he had heard his British masters speak wistfully of rose and honeysuckle in Hampshire, but somehow the word seemed inappropriate for the functional tin-roofed structure in which the Karanjas took their leave.

'How are things at home?' asked bin Seyd. 'Family all right?'

'Very well, thank you. Grace has been under the weather again, but she's better now. She wouldn't go to the doctor. You know what she's like.'

'The boys?'

'They're away at the moment. At school. James is at Wellington now. He's doing very well.' There was pride in his voice.

'And your younger son?' bin Seyd struggled to remember the name.

'Stephen. He's still at Haggard Hall. He's taking the common entrance next term.'

Again Karanja spoke with pride, but also with a slight unease. Haggard Hall was a Kenya prep school, an exclusive establishment to which all the aristocratic white settlers sent their sons. Stephen Karanja was one of half a dozen token black boys accepted into the school at the same time as the photograph of Sir Winston Churchill in the dining hall was replaced with one of Jomo Kenyatta. Karanja senior was happy to see his son in such a place. Like all sensitive parents however, he also experienced occasional feelings of guilt. He missed his boy around the house. Letters from Stephen were few and far between, but always distant, always slightly impersonal. There had been one recently which he had not entirely understood, and it had disturbed him.

The letter was in his pocket now. Karanja took it out and read it again: '*We beat Pembroke House two-one last week. I got five lines for ragging. Major Gale says he will beat me if I do it again. Smith-Baggot's flamingo has died.*'

There was more, but Karanja did not read on. He handed the letter to bin Seyd and tapped it with his finger. 'There. What do you make of that? *Ragging?*'

The dictionary had not been illuminating. *Ragging: to rebuke, scold, tease, torment, make hay of (person's room etc), indulge in horseplay, engage in ballyragging, spree; lark, play rough jokes on.* Karanja was a cultivated man; he appreciated that English is a language of idiom. He knew also that he could never be a party to the intimate argot of the English boarding school. Nevertheless the idea of his son making hay of someone's room struck him as unlikely. Reading between the lines – Stephen had warned him that letters were censored – he wondered if there was not something going on that he ought to know about, that was being deliberately kept from him.

'I don't understand it,' said bin Seyd, returning the letter. 'Really it's most unusual.'

From across the island – Mombasa is an island – came the

familiar chuntering sound of the night train to Nairobi. Usually Karanja was pleased to hear it, for it meant that he could decently order a drink from the bar. Since the withdrawal of the British it would have been a foolish man who attempted to set his watch by the train's departure, but the sound was nevertheless a comforting one, a reassuring tradition in a restless world. In the early years of the century, when the train had set off uncertainly on a journey to nowhere in particular, it had been derided as the lunatic express. Nowadays it enjoyed a certain prestige as one of the last romantic railway journeys of the age. From Mombasa it led across the causeway to the mainland proper, the gateway to Africa, and for the next eight hundred miles pursued a hazardous course across a land resonant with the old names of empire. The man-eaters of Tsavo; the snows of Kilimanjaro; the flame trees of Thika. Nairobi, home to a pair of English Dukes, paramount chiefs both; Naivasha, where Sir Henry Rider Haggard had set much of his fiction and where, even now, Stephen Karanja risked a thrashing at Haggard Hall. The Rift Valley, which splits the world from the Holy Land to Mozambique; Happy Valley, where the ten commandments had never penetrated. Up nine thousand feet and down again across the equator to the mimosas of Lake Victoria – eight hundred miles of swamp and desert, jungle and plain, a journey like no other in the world.

'Late again, the train,' said bin Seyd happily. Between the smartly uniformed Kenya Police and the civilians of the Railways and Harbours Board there was a mutual contempt inherited, as so much else, from the British.

'I wonder sometimes what does go on at Haggard Hall,' said Karanja. 'My boy won't tell me. Whenever I ask him he just clams up, says I wouldn't understand.'

Across the island, the train let out a series of toots as it reached the causeway. The journey had begun. Thus had it tooted for Edward, Prince of Wales and his American mistress Lady Furness; for Winston Churchill and Theodore Roosevelt; for Hemingway, Blixen, Huxley and Ruark; and for all the younger sons, the aristocrats in disgrace, some to remain in exile for ever, others to reappear after only a few weeks, hurrying home to write a book

13

with *Lion*, *Safari* or *Masai* in the title. Towards the same time
tomorrow — assuming no elephants on the line, locusts in the
engine, floods, bush fires or even *shauri ya Mungu*, the will of God
— the train would be approaching Naivasha, six thousand feet up in
what had once been the White Highlands; and from his classroom
Stephen Karanja would hear it in the distance, as his father heard
it now.

Karanja's thoughts went with the train as it crossed to the mainland. Usually at this time he would be squirming round in his chair
to catch the barman's eye — but not tonight. He had something
else to do. Instead of a drink he called for pen and paper. He was
going to write to Haggard Hall. The headmaster's name was Gale.
Karanja wanted to hear from Desmond Gale. He wanted to find
out more, everything a parent ought to know, about *ragging*.

2

'Cats on the rooftops, cats on the tiles,
Cats with syphilis, cats with piles,
Cats. . . .'

'Hey!'

'Sir?'

'You there, Karanja. Was that you singing that song?'

'Yes sir.' Stephen Karanja searched for the headmaster and found him looking out of his study window.

'Where did you learn language like that?'

'From Lord Byron, sir. The poet.'

'I know who Byron was.' Forty years ago Desmond had sung the same song at bump suppers. 'But who taught it to you?'

'Mr Waterhouse did. Before he left.'

'Well you're to forget it, do you hear? Forget all about it. Cats with syphilis! I've never heard anything so revolting.'

'Animals do get it, sir. And gonorrhoea. Mr Waterhouse said in Borneo the natives went to bed with orang-utangs and they all died of clap. The orangs, that is.'

Desmond Gale was a tall man, about six foot two. His eyes were a deep blue, his hair white and distinguished. He had the nose and moustache of an old warrior. When he chose to bristle, the effect could be intimidating. He bristled now.

'Do you know the factors of nineteen?'

Stephen looked blank.

'Go away and find out. I shall ask you at tea.'

Desmond watched sourly as Karanja disappeared. Mr Waterhouse had a lot to answer for. During his short time at Haggard Hall there had been a noticeable decline in discipline – less

15

formality, the young man had called it – among the junior boys. The problem would have to be remedied.

Desmond returned to his seat. The morning post had just been delivered on horseback, and his desk was piled high with the usual correspondence of headmasters: letters from parents – including one from Karanja's father about ragging, which he did not intend to answer – bills, reports, prospectuses, application forms for English public schools, a never-ending stream of information kept heavily in place by a copy of Burke's Peerage. Of Desmond's own volumes, only a leather-bound fishing book was allowed to remain on the desk. The others lined a glass case over his gun rack. Behind the door there was an elephant's foot umbrella stand in which he kept his cane, bamboo fishing rods, a Wakamba hunting-bow strung so tight that none of the boys could pull it, and various weapons of war – a knobkerrie, a Masai spear and the ceremonial stabbing sword of the Grenadier Guards, engraved with the major battle honours on the blade and his initials on the hilt. To this in fact he was entitled, having been conscripted briefly into the Brigade of Guards at the end of the war. Otherwise the room contained little decoration except a rowing photograph of himself at the House and a print of a racehorse his grandfather had once owned.

'Sorry about that, Padre,' he apologised. 'Awful little boy. Now, where were we?'

The Padre was a rubicund man of bespectacled middle age who had first come out to Kenya as chaplain to the King's African Rifles. During his subsequent career teaching English and Divinity, the name had always stuck.

'Smith-Baggot, headmaster.'

'Yes, Smith-Baggot.' Desmond waved a letter. 'His results have come from Eton. *Not* very good, I'm afraid. They posted his name on the college gates. He failed.'

'Any chance of trying again next term?'

'They don't think so.'

The Padre was not surprised. 'He'll have to be told.'

'I thought actually you might like to do it, Padre. Comfort of the church, and all that. Where is he now?'

16

'In the san, headmaster. He ate a whole flamingo.'

There had been a wounded flamingo on the playing fields, a fugitive from Lake Naivasha. Trailing a broken leg, it had arrived one afternoon during a game of football and had been enthusiastically adopted by Smith-Baggot. In fact the flamingo had been managing perfectly well on the other leg, was well on the way to recovery until Smith-Baggot began to care for it. Thereafter it had died and Smith-Baggot, with the unsentimentality of youth, had eaten it. He came of an old settler family, steeped in the pioneer virtues of improvisation and self-help. After plucking the feathers, useful for the headmaster's fly-tying class, he had boiled the carcass and eaten it at one sitting. Now he was in the sanatorium.

'I'd better go and break it to him,' said the Padre.

'You might let his parents know while you're about it. They won't be very pleased. They were rather counting on getting him in to Eton.'

Desmond's study was in the east wing of the Hall. From one window he had an uninterrupted view of Lake Naivasha, from the other an oblique glimpse of the extinct volcano Mount Longonot. On a good day it was sometimes possible to see hippo, zebra and giraffe at the same time, though never in great numbers any more. The first white man to push through the Rift Valley, a Scot named Thomson, had reported thousands of zebra along the shores of the lake – but that was a hundred years ago. Thomson had also reported thousands of Masai warriors, whom he terrified by removing his false teeth. When he returned to England his exploits were adapted by a young lawyer named Henry Rider Haggard, first in *King Solomon's Mines*, later in *She*. Ayesha, the central figure of *She*, ruled a volcanic domain lifted entirely from Thomson's description of Longonot; it was to this that Haggard Hall owed its name.

The Hall had not always been a school. It had originally been built in the 1920s as a private house, a more or less faithful replica of Lord Dunsinane's family seat in the lowlands of Scotland. Lord Dunsinane had come out to Kenya after the Great War to shoot big game; he had stayed to farm and chase women. With much of Scotland at his disposal – together with a good part of the industrial Midlands by one of his earlier marriages – he had been able to build a grand mock-Tudor house to his own specification, with eighteenth century additions. There was a baronial dining hall at one end, lit by a double storeyed bay window looking square on to the lake, and a baronial drawing room – now a dormitory – the other. The fireplace in what was now the staff room could seat a dozen in comfort, and the double front door – a gift from the Sultan of Zanzibar as one aristocrat to another – was magnificently studded with Arab brass. The roof trusses were of a Tudor design, carefully distorted to look old (to the mystification of the Indian *fundi* who had put them in); the oriel windows gleamed with heraldic glass. Lord Dunsinane had firm views on what sort of house an Englishman abroad could live in. Haggard Hall was just such a house.

Unfortunately he had not survived long to enjoy his surroundings, for the collapse of his health – a combination of drink, drugs, sexual excess and blackwater fever – had coincided with the farming slump of 1931 to drive him out of his mind. Lord Dunsinane had been a leading member of the Happy Valley set in his day. He had opted for a life of adultery and improvidence, of fast living at high altitude, and had paid the price. One afternoon in 1932 – penniless, sick, alone – he had loaded a rifle in the front hall and shot first his red setter, then himself.

Now all that remained of the lotus eaters who had once rampaged through the house was a photograph of Lord Dunsinane in swimsuit and solar topee, and a flagstone in the hall – shown to all new boys their first day – where the body had been discovered. For several years after his death the Hall had been a fishing hotel, a regular stopping place for anyone venturing north from Nairobi. Evelyn Waugh stayed there when it was still a private house; Hemingway camped, amid much fanfare, in the grounds. Both recorded the experience, Waugh in his diary: *Stayed night Haggard Hall. Hideous Gothic pile. Host Lord Dunsinane, also Joss Erroll and sluttish girl named ——. Erroll woke me up in middle of night to tell me had just put cocaine on penis.* Hemingway in a letter home: *I wish you could see this place, Dan. The sky so high and the hills all kind of bluey gray and the air fresh and clear with a kick like a good Martini, the ones Pilar used to make. The spears long and slim, the sweet grass stiff with buck, the Somali girls all doe-eyed with kohl. And the big ones, Dan. Lion, rhino, chui the leopard. A man could find himself in country like this.*

A man could. But not even Hemingway managed to save Haggard Hall from the Depression. In 1936 the hotel went into liquidation and was sold for a prep school. Thus had it remained ever since, shakily at first, then with growing confidence as prosperity returned to Kenya's settlers. Its honours board since the war boasted a muted number of scholarships to English public schools, its sporting trophies a keen athleticism. Latin was on the curriculum, for without it a curriculum would have had no meaning. There were three houses – Gagool, Umbopa, Quatermain – bath nights twice a week, covert renderings of *God save the Queen* on special occasions.

Smith-Baggot took the news of his failure calmly. Five years at Haggard Hall had taught him to conceal his feelings. He was in any case too ill to express much emotion either way, for a flamingo is not an edible bird. He simply listened weakly as the Padre attempted to comfort him.

'There are other schools, you know. Plenty to choose from.'

'Yes sir.'

'It's not the end of the world.'

'No sir.'

'You must take the common entrance again next term. We shall coach you.'

'Yes sir. Thank you, sir.'

Smith-Baggot tried to look interested, but his mind was elsewhere. He had never been to England. He had no interest in anything much beyond the animals of his parents' farm. Privately he wished that the Padre would go away. This, after a few minutes, the Padre did.

Letting himself out of a side door, he headed across the lawn to a tall wooden structure on a slight rise overlooking the playing fields. The structure was an old watch tower left over from the Mau Mau emergency. Since the Padre's arrival it had been converted into a home for his personal hobby, carrier pigeons. Pigeons and pigeon racing are a proletarian sport in England, but in Kenya they were far from being a sport at all. Many parts of the country had no telephone link with the outside world, and although there was an erratic line at Naivasha it had never extended as far as Haggard Hall. Short of a trip into town on one of the days when the phone was working, the only swift means of communication was via the Padre's pigeons, of which some fifty or sixty nested in boxes at the top of a ten foot ladder.

Puffing with exertion, the Padre climbed the tower and swung himself into the loft. He had brought a supply of maize cobs in a bucket and a change of water. During the moult the birds would need green vegetables and cod liver oil from the sanatorium; during the cricket season, linseed oil to keep their feathers in trim. But sudden changes of diet were bad for them – for most of the year he liked to keep them on a regime of pure cereal.

Soon his head and shoulders were lost to view as the birds fought for a share of the maize. The Padre crowed with pleasure. He was proud of his birds. Each had a name, a page to itself in his notebook, a history of its every illness – egg binding, croup, canker of the throat. He took his hobby seriously.

On one side of the door, a little apart from the other boxes, stood a single wicker cage marked in white paint *Smith-Baggot*. From inside the Padre withdrew a small racing Homer, a stranger to the loft. Clutching the Homer to his chest, he fought off the other birds and stepped to the outside rail, from where he could see across a corner of Lake Naivasha to the distant magnificence of the Aberdare mountains beyond. The Smith-Baggots lived on a farm only seventy miles away, but separated from Haggard Hall by the impassable 13,000 foot range of the Aberdares. When they came to visit their son, it was by private aeroplane.

REGRET FAILED ETON. Sending a message by carrier pigeon always made the Padre feel good, like Caesar in Gaul, a Crusader smiting the Saracens. With his free hand he attached the message

20

to the ring on the bird's leg and glinted skywards, searching for a hawk. There were none about. Gripping the bird with both hands, he chose his moment and heaved it into the sky.

The bird fluttered uncertainly on the breeze, then took off low in the direction of the mountains. The Padre watched it go. Within two hours, all being well, it would reach its destination on the plains of Naro Moru. Not for the first time that day the Padre wondered whether it would brave the altitude in direct flight, or whether it would choose to fly around the mountains instead. If ever he found the answer to that question, he had promised himself he would write a short paper about it for one of the English ornithological journals.

3

'About Mr Waterhouse,' said Desmond. Mr Waterhouse had been a young man from England, a young man with a beard. He had been asked to leave not for the usual reason, but for a divergence of political philosophy. Mr Waterhouse had gone barefoot and talked about the need for a less structured approach in the classroom. He had used words like cool and hassle. Desmond had got rid of him.

'What about Mr Waterhouse?' asked the Padre warily.

'Now he's gone there's no one to teach geometry.'

'Headmaster, I know nothing about geometry.'

'Or algebra to the lower boys.'

'I can't teach geometry, headmaster.'

'Nonsense, Padre, of course you can. Just tell them about similar triangles. Concyclic points. It's all in the book.'

The Padre was bitter. They had had this conversation before. There had been a succession of young men out from England. Older ones too. For the schoolmastering profession, up-country Kenya was often the end of the line.

'Couldn't you ask Mr Nodleman?' he pleaded. Eugene Nodleman, a graduate student from America, taught geography part time.

'Nodleman has agreed to teach algebra. But only if you'll tackle geometry.'

'I didn't know he could teach algebra?'

'He can't. But he's agreed to learn.'

The Padre capitulated. He always knew when he was beaten. 'I suppose I could cover for a while,' he conceded. 'If it has to be done. But only for a while, headmaster. You must get someone else in before the end of term.'

'Good man.' Desmond handed him a set square. 'You can take the common entrance form after break. I knew I could depend on you.'

'Nodleman,' said Desmond ten minutes later. 'The Padre has offered to take on geometry for the moment. It might be a gesture under the circumstances if you would agree to teach algebra. Just for a while, at least.'

'Sure,' nodded Eugene. 'Why not?'

4

Desmond Gale had come late to schoolmastering and by a circuitous route. Nor had he spent much time in the army, although his claim to the rank of major was perfectly genuine. For most of his life he had been an adventurer, of a type well known in Kenya. He had arrived in the colony almost by accident, a penniless young man, attempting to work his passage to Australia as a professional gambler aboard an ocean liner. The captain had requested him to leave the ship at Port Said; he had eventually left it at Port Sudan, but only with the intention of reboarding at Mombasa. Stranded meantime in the Sudan, he had made his way inland to Khartoum, where he spent the larger part of his winnings on a single air ticket to Kenya.

In those days – this was 1949 – there was no international airport at Nairobi. The Imperial Airways service to East Africa via Augusta, Alexandria and Khartoum was by flying boat. It was from the porthole of a Solent that Desmond first set eyes on Kenya, having joined the flight at Khartoum. The plane – boat – landed on Lake Naivasha within sight of Haggard Hall, although Desmond did not realise it until later. The rest of the journey was completed first by motor boat to the shore, then overland for the remaining forty miles to Nairobi, an exotic form of travel, one which exactly suited Desmond's taste for the outlandish.

As they approached the shore at the end of the flight, Desmond could make out a number of cameramen on the jetty waiting to photograph their arrival. At first he assumed this was normal procedure, as it was when passenger ships came in to port. But it soon became obvious that the boat was carrying a couple of out-of-the-ordinary passengers in Stewart Granger and Deborah Kerr, who had journeyed from England to make the film version of *King*

Solomon's Mines. Desmond wasted no time. A photograph of the couple appeared next day on the front page of the *East African Standard*; it featured the two film stars and between them Desmond Gale, a young ex-Guards officer who had been their travelling companion on the flight.

Desmond lived off the incident for months after his arrival. In the minds of the settler community – especially the women – he became ineradicably linked with the glamorous world of the movies. He talked often of Stewart and Debo, doing little to countermand the impression that he had an important job on the film set, and found a credulous audience among the memsahibs and remittance men of Nairobi. The colony's blue-bloods took him into their midst – as they took every eligible newcomer. They gave him the run of their guest cottages and saw to it that he was put up for the Muthaiga Club. In a short time Desmond knew everyone who was anyone in Nairobi. The Australian liner came and went, but he made no effort to rejoin it, for he had fallen a willing victim to his new surroundings. His instinct for survival, always strong, told him that in Kenya he would recapture the lazy charm of his formative years. His formative years had been Anglo-Irish – he had been brought up to a world of horses, large houses and charming, feckless natives. In Kenya, as in the Ireland of his youth, he recognised life as it ought to be.

In Kenya, as in Ireland, the natives were not so sure. The Mau Mau years followed swiftly on his arrival and Desmond, as a single man of military age, was one of the first to be called up into the Kenya Regiment. It was in the Kenya Regiment – rather than the Grenadiers whose tie he wore – that he had been a major. But the soldiering was fun. In fact Desmond always remembered the Emergency as the best time of his life. The other side put up a miserable performance, armed only with pangas and home-made rifles. Desmond for his part did just enough fighting to experience a keen sense of exhilaration and acquire a fund of stories; the rest of the time he patrolled the European suburbs of Nairobi with an ostrich feather in his hat, a revolver on each hip and a supporting arm for the wives of comrades who were away in the hills for weeks at a time.

They were good years for Desmond, more so than the years which followed. Before the call-up his only experience of work had been a stint as farm manager to a man he had met in the Outspan bar at Nyeri. After his demob he tried his hand at a variety of different jobs – club secretary, racehorse trainer, organiser of big game safaris – each with less success than the last. He was not suited to any form of business. As the winds of change blew and black rule in Kenya became inevitable, he gave up all pretence of earning a living and decided to seek pastures new. He had no money in Kenya, no reason to stay, nothing to lose by going. Nairobi was a nervous town in the run-up to independence and Desmond shared the general unease. There were also recriminations between him and a settler's ex-wife who had been refused an invitation to meet royalty at Government House on account of her divorce. She blamed Desmond for this snub and he, in a rare moment of introspection, agreed. It was time for him to go.

Word went out to his friends, who clubbed together to send him back to England. Several hundred of them attended a farewell party at the Norfolk hotel, applauding vigorously as his great crony the Duke of Manchester presented him with a silver salver – bought cheap at one of the many farm auctions then taking place – and a sizeable cheque intended to buy him an airline ticket to London-Heathrow. Desmond accepted the money gratefully. He made a suitably appreciative speech of thanks and used the cheque to slip across the border to Uganda, where he sold the salver and quietly established himself in one of the leafier suburbs of Kampala until he had time to think out his next move.

In fact he had already made his next move, although he did not immediately appreciate it, for it was in Uganda that his luck began to change. The dice had rolled again, this time in Desmond's favour. It so happened that the British administration maintained a puppet king in Kampala in the person of Sir Edward Mutesa, hereditary chief of the Baganda tribe, a Cambridge-educated potentate whose life was dedicated to women and drink, not necessarily in that order. During his younger days King Freddie (as he was known) had proved so difficult to handle that the British had been forced to remove him from Uganda for his own good. They had also given him a commission in the Grenadier Guards, the obvious choice for a monarch of good standing. It did not take Desmond long to introduce himself to His Majesty as the local representative of the Old Comrades association – a move he knew in advance would be welcome because King Freddie had fond memories of his former regiment, whose height and plumed headdresses reminded him of his own household warriors. He and Desmond hit it off from the first.

To the annoyance of the British administrators appointed to the task, Desmond swiftly installed himself as an unofficial adviser to the king, a power behind the throne whose word – though without any legal authority – became a force to be reckoned with. The rules of the game had long ago been established to the satisfaction of the British. Now they began to change. Protocol, the umbrella protection of entrenched, well-ordered procedures, became a thing of the past – at least as far as Desmond was concerned. Although he was their puppet, King Freddie's colonial advisers had always treated him with proper deference, as befitted his station. Now they found themselves edged out by Desmond, whose lack of decorum was soon the despair of Government House. When the British entered the royal presence they dressed from force of habit in suit and tie, and came prepared to discuss important matters of state. Now, more often than not, they found Desmond already there in shirtsleeves, a drink in one hand, a cigarette in the other. The British treated Freddie as a monarch, albeit a dark one. Desmond treated him as a subaltern in the mess. More and more Freddie turned to Desmond, a man who gave him no aggravation, for companionship and advice.

Naturally it could not last. Independence came, the British departed, the people of Uganda became responsible again for their own destiny. The majority of them rose up in fury against the dominance of the Baganda tribe. There was a massacre in the streets of Kampala, the first of many. King Freddie escaped to England, where he died in obscurity some years later. Desmond slipped over the palace wall at the first sign of trouble and drove through the night to the Kenyan frontier. Several parties of drunken soldiers tried to block his path, but he stopped for nothing and no one. He reached Nairobi next day in a borrowed Mercedes, dapper as ever, with a fortune in East African currency – gifts to the king from his Asian contractors, entrusted to Desmond for safekeeping – hidden inside the spare wheel. He was safe; and for the first time in his life, comfortably off.

But the experience had shaken him more than he cared to admit. Although he enjoyed his reputation as a wild man, the incident of the palace wall lingered uncomfortably in his memory, for Desmond had been near enough to hear the dying screams of the Bagandans as the mob closed in. He himself had escaped with only minutes to spare. In retrospect it made a wonderful story, and he told it often at the bar of the New Stanley ('I was scared stiff, old man! Believe me! Scared absolutely rigid!'). But at the time Desmond had been genuinely terrified. He had seen his hands tremble, had felt his legs shaking. He knew, deep down, that he no longer needed the sort of excitement a massacre could provide.

So it was in an uncharacteristically pessimistic mood – a recognition perhaps of early middle age – that Desmond came upon Haggard Hall. The school was up for sale; he was in a position to buy it. He knew little about schoolmastering and cared less; but there was something about the Hall itself, one of the grandest houses in Kenya, that appealed to his patrician instincts. It was a fine place to live. There were horses in the stable and streams in the Aberdares amply stocked with trout. School terms were not as long as they might be, and during the holidays he could play the country squire, a role that suited him well. He could live like a settler with none of the bother of farming. Really it might have been made for him. Emptying out the spare wheel, he put down the money for the property, sent off a cheque to Oxford for his MA, and became Desmond Gale, Headmaster.

There he had remained ever since. The school continued to prosper, and so did Desmond. At the beginning, mindful of the good impression a wife made on prospective parents, he caught the settler's ex-wife between lovers and married her. The marriage lasted five years and after their divorce they remained on good terms. Desmond had lived alone ever since, although his attraction to women had diminished little with age. To his great satisfaction he was still as healthy and vigorous as a forty-year-old.

He was also consolidating his reputation as one of the community's established celebrities, for tales of his exploits were circulated more and more often as time moved on, and not always by him. The European population of Kenya had suffered a dramatic change in the years after independence. The original pioneers had largely died out or retreated elsewhere, to be replaced by a new breed of businessmen – two year wonders – who came out on short-term contracts and then returned to Surbiton to show off their slides. For these pale beings the old Kenya was simply a legend. They could not tell the difference between Desmond and the genuine article. They knew him only as a *mzee*, a senior member of the Muthaiga Club, a link with the exotic past. When he entered the Club on one of his increasingly rare visits to Nairobi – dressed in safari clothes and spotted green cravat; covered in the dust of up-country; looking down his nose at anyone who had not been 'out here' as long as he had – they nudged each other and pointed him out as an old time settler, one of those extraordinary characters who had really opened up this most extraordinary of countries. 'Grand old boy,' they told each other in awed whispers. 'Incredible chap. Absolutely incredible. You won't see anyone like him again.' Desmond agreed with them.

5

For two weeks the Padre fulfilled his bargain with Desmond and taught geometry to the boys of the common entrance form. He found the experience unsettling.

'We know about Pythagoras,' Karanja told him, 'The square on the hypotenuse is equal to the sum of the squares on the other two sides. We know all that, sir. It's the converse we don't understand.'

'The converse?'

'If the square on one side of a triangle is equal to the sum of the squares on the other two sides, then the angle between those two sides is a right angle. How do you prove that, sir?'

At the end of two weeks, his heart filled with un-Christian rage, the Padre presented himself in Desmond's doorway.

'It's no good, headmaster. I can't do it any more. I can't teach geometry, not to the common entrance boys, not to anyone. I simply can't do it.'

There was an edge to his voice that Desmond affected not to notice.

'Padre. Just the man. Hold this, would you?' Desmond was a person of few hobbies, but one of them was fly-tying. His study was littered with abandoned flies in various stages of completion. He was working now on a dry fly made from feathers supplied by Smith-Baggot. Still simmering, the Padre took one end of a piece of thread.

'I wonder if it isn't a bit gaudy?' Desmond mused. 'Pink, I mean. Trout aren't used to flamingo. Might frighten them off.'

'Headmaster.' The Padre was in anguish. 'You must find a replacement for Mr Waterhouse. You really must. You can't expect me to carry on like this.'

'Would it help if I gave you an increase in salary?' Twenty per cent of Mr Waterhouse's wages would still leave Desmond with a saving of eighty.

'No headmaster, you've missed the point. Money has nothing to do with it. I simply don't want to teach geometry. English is what I teach. And Divinity.'

'It isn't easy, you know, getting a replacement. I shall have to write to England. It will take time.'

'I don't mind how much time it takes. Just so long as someone comes.'

The Padre was serious. Desmond had suspected it all along. 'All right,' he conceded. 'All right, Padre. I'll see what can be done.' He tied another knot and held up the fly for inspection. 'I shall write to England today.'

'Thank you, headmaster.'

'Mind you, we'll still have to give it some thought. We must be careful who we choose. Waterhouse wore a chain round his neck. We don't want another one like that.'

'Indeed not.'

'They send out a different type of young man from England these days. I don't know where they get their ideas from. Full of nonsense about Kenya being a part of the Third World, as if they know what that means. No use to us here. Not what we need at all.'

In view of his pathetic results from Eton, details of which were already being gleefully discussed by the others in his form, Smith-Baggot had made up his mind to run away from Haggard Hall as soon as the chance arose. He did not take the decision lightly, for running away in Africa was a dangerous business, but he calculated that anything would be preferable to staying on at school. He was a lonely boy, always more at ease in the company of animals than people. From his grandparents, who had been among the first Europeans to settle in Kenya, he had inherited a taste for freedom and a love of open spaces which the confines of Haggard Hall entirely failed to satisfy. He wanted to go home, to the wide plains and eddying streams of Naro Moru, where no one knew about the

31

ablative absolute and no one cared. The day after his release from the sick room, he began to plan his escape.

Escaping from Haggard Hall presented certain problems, for the main buildings were surrounded by a thick barbed wire fence erected during the Mau Mau troubles and never subsequently removed. Originally the fence had been connected to a mild electric current, until a previous headmaster discovered the prefects forcing smaller boys to pee onto it. Since then it had served as a climbing frame for a *kei*-apple hedge. It had two gates, one leading to the gravelled front drive, the other to a distant collection of huts which housed the servants and their families. Near this back exit stood the Padre's pigeon loft cum watch tower; beside it a battery of floodlights which illuminated the approaches after dark. The overall effect, inevitably, was of a prison camp: it was in the Colditz tradition that Smith-Baggot contemplated his escape.

Like most Kenyans he had little interest in books and was scornful of people who preferred to read when they could be outside killing things. But there was one book in the school library that he had read again and again – Felice Benuzzi's *No Picnic on Mount Kenya*, a moving account of three Italian prisoners of war who had broken out of camp in 1943 in order to climb Kenya's highest mountain. The story was a classic one of courage and daring; it had taken hold of Smith-Baggot's somewhat limited imagination. He longed to emulate the feat.

His troubles, he knew, would be only just beginning outside the wire. The only practical way home lay straight across the Aberdare mountains, ten thousand feet at their most negotiable, a chilling wilderness of forest, bamboo and moorland. To reach the treeline at the foot of the Aberdares he would first have to cross a dozen miles or so of open veld, much of it in full view of the watch tower at Haggard Hall. This was the dangerous part. Once inside the forest he would be comparatively safe, for it would be almost impossible for any pursuers to track him down. Smith-Baggot had enough confidence in his own bushcraft to feel sure of reaching the saddle of the mountains without mishap – and so down the other side to the grasslands of Naro Moru. He would travel along elephant paths and game trails, just as the Masai had done before their surprise raids on the Kikuyu. If the game trails failed he would find a stream and follow it upwards to its source. Only in the last resort would he traverse the mountains' single official road – a scarcely discernible mud track, impassable in wet weather, used solely by game wardens and suitably equipped safari vehicles.

The Aberdares are a national park, and the forest in his path was stiff with buffalo and rhino. Once over the other side he would skirt the elephant lick at Treetops, where garish women in leopardskin coats terrified the baboons. Yet Smith-Baggot was not deterred. He was a resourceful boy, small for his age but determined. He had already gathered his equipment for the expedition – a compass, a waterproof torch, and a bush knife which he had used to cut the throat of a Thomson's gazelle which had unwisely strayed across the school boundary at the bottom of the playing fields. The Tommy would provide all the food he needed for the trip. After hanging the carcass to drain the blood, he had sliced the flesh into long strips to dry in the sun. The resultant biltong should keep long enough to get him safely over the mountains.

Besides the knife, his only other dependable weapon was a rifle. As a member of the sharp-shooting team he was allowed to keep his .22 sporting rifle at school, chained to the gun rack in Desmond's study. It could be removed either with a hacksaw (noisy) or a key. Smith-Baggot knew that the key was kept in the right hand drawer of Desmond's desk; he was confident, when the time came, of retrieving it unnoticed. A more difficult problem was ammunition, for Desmond kept the cartridge boxes under tight control. He was fond of reminding boys that it was a court martial offence to remove live rounds from the firing range. Nonetheless Smith-Baggot had managed to steal five. They were concealed now in his inkwell.

The only remaining difficulty was one of timing. When to escape – night or day? Smith-Baggot weighed up the options. On balance he decided for dawn, when vitality was at its lowest and the night watchman's guard would be down. No one would miss him then if he was careful. It was all a question of timing. As long as he slipped through the wire unnoticed, he would be okay. He would be away and into the trees. Till then, the thing to do was to keep his head down and wait.

'The trouble is the agency,' said Desmond. 'We write to the agency and what do we get? Waterhouse. And before him they sent us the one who couldn't drive, and the one who got headaches from the altitude; and before them the one who didn't drink. It's the agency that's the trouble.'

'Perhaps another agent, headmaster. . . .'

'They're all the same, though. They all have the same people on their books. It's a vicious circle. Once you've tried one you've tried them all.'

'An advertisement then. In one of the newspapers.'

'You know what I think? I think the job calls for a military man. You and me, Padre, we're military men. We know the form. We know how to handle the livestock. Not like the people they send out nowadays.'

'You mean an old soldier?'

'Something of the kind. Someone – anyone – who doesn't have ideas of his own, who can stand up to the boys. It's no joke running a school like this in the middle of nowhere. You know it, Padre. *I* know it. But they don't seem to know it in England.'

'I suppose there is something in what you say, headmaster. An army officer would certainly know the ropes. A man with experience.'

'Too much to hope for a decent regiment, I should think. Still, you can never tell.'

'A suitably worded advertisement might yield results.' The Padre was warming to the idea. 'Ex-army officer seeks challenging position. That sort of thing.'

'Be careful how you write it, Padre. I rely on you. I think you know that.'

The Padre did. Somehow he always seemed to end up writing Desmond's letters for him. He was a placid man, but as he walked

34

down the corridor to his room he could not restrain a momentary feeling of irritation at Desmond's behaviour. As so often, the Padre considered that he had been left to hold the fort.

The Padre's room was on the ground floor of the Hall, overlooking the rose garden. It had been his room for many years and he had furnished it a trifle fussily, according to the tastes of a middle-aged bachelor. Apart from a sister in Kent whom he had not seen for twenty years, there had never been a woman in the Padre's life; nor, oddly for a parson in his position, any little boys. His life had been dedicated to institutions, first the King's African Rifles – where he had known Idi Amin, the only famous man he had ever met – latterly Haggard Hall, where he congratulated himself that some hundreds of boys had successfully passed on to English schools as a result of his teaching.

There were few overt signs of religion in the room, for the Padre's faith was of the passive, unreflective kind. He had long ago forgotten his reasons for becoming a parson. Apart from his vestments on the back of the door, the only hint of his calling was a Bible on the bookshelf, tucked in between a pair of nesting boxes and a much-thumbed copy of *The Screwtape Letters*. The Padre taught Divinity and preached the sermon on Sundays; his only other religious duties were extra-curricular, for he helped out occasionally at a newly founded Protestant mission just outside Naivasha. The mission had been set up to combat the influence of the Catholic Church – in the form of two Irish priests and an Italian – who touted for business in a wooden assembly hall a few miles away across the veld. The Padre was not anti-Catholic as such – he welcomed the ecumenical movement – but he believed vaguely that anyone who spoke English, as the Africans all did, had a logical obligation to belong to the Church of England. In all other respects he took his pastoral duties lightly.

The Padre's chair was by the window. Unlacing his boots, he made himself a cup of tea and sat down with pencil and paper to compose an advertisement for the English newspapers. The post was collected every afternoon at 4.30, when an African syce took it on horseback to Naivasha in time for the down-train to Nairobi. The Padre was anxious to get the letter off before Desmond changed his mind. He was thus engaged when Eugene Nodleman looked in.

'Hi Padre. How you doing? You want to see what I got today?'

Without waiting for a reply, Eugene came in and sat on the bed. The Padre shifted his chair reluctantly. Eugene was a graduate student of about thirty-four, in between grants at the moment, who taught at Haggard Hall while completing the field work for a dissertation of unrelieved complexity. He wore dark glasses, a beard and a mass of tight curly hair, but was allowed to get away with it because he had undertaken to organise the sporting programme for the season. He was dressed now in jogging shorts and a tee shirt with *Tufts* written across the front.

Slipping off his rucksack, Eugene rummaged inside and laid out the fruit of the day's labours on the bed – a thigh bell, a cattle amulet, a tape recorder and a tape cassette labelled *Masai 108*.

'I got them to do it for me,' he told the Padre. 'I finally did.'

He played the recording. An indecipherable wailing filled the room, accompanied by the sound of shuffling feet and various unexplained thumps at irregular intervals. Eugene listened for fifteen minutes, tapping his pen against his teeth, shooting triumphant glances at the Padre, before switching it off.

'A lion dance,' he explained.

'That's wonderful,' said the Padre.

'If I'd only known, you know. Only I didn't take my movie camera with me. I left it behind. I thought it was going to be all just talk today.'

The Padre tut-tutted.

'That's what I really need to do. To get all the Masai dance routines on film. A complete record of the basic steps before they disappear.'

'Mostly I think they just jump up and down, don't they?'

'Pardon me?'

'It was just a thought,' said the Padre.

Eugene pressed the rewind button. 'I guess I'm beginning to win the tribe's confidence at last,' he went on. 'That's because they can see how I relate to them. They're teaching me so much about myself that I never knew before. After the rains they're going to let me watch them eat meat. An *olpul*. That's kind of an honour, because it's only the warriors that get to eat meat. Special occasions only. They can't do it in the village, or any place where women might see them. They have a secret hideout in the hills.'

Once, in an unguarded moment, the Padre had asked Eugene what his doctoral thesis was about. Eugene had told him. The Padre had listened for fifty minutes, without getting a word in edgeways, and had come away little the wiser. The thesis was loosely entitled *Aspects of Masai ethnoculture in the post-colonial era: a study in symbiotic nomadism* to conceal a certain doubt in Eugene's own mind, for he had been unable to identify beyond question a line of inquiry not already claimed by one of the scores of American anthropologists who roamed the plains in search of academic tenure. All he knew for certain was that it would be about the Masai, because it had been a photograph of a warrior *manyatta* in *Life* magazine that had brought him to Africa in the first place. After reading the accompanying article he had booked a flight to Kenya and requested an introduction to the Masai through the Ministry of Education in Nairobi. The ensuing meeting at the Thorn Tree café with a trio of polite, if puzzled, young men in collars and ties – one of them with an AB from Harvard – had only momentarily disconcerted him. These, he swiftly realised, were not the real Masai. He plunged off at once into the bush in pursuit of ethnicity. Thus he came to Haggard Hall.

Although there was plenty of room at the Hall, Eugene had always refused the offer of his own bedroom in the main building. He preferred to get the real feel of the *bundu* by living in a tent a hundred yards away across the tennis court. A famous photograph exists of Ernest Hemingway at Naivasha, in authentic white hunter garb, staring resolutely into the harsh middle distance of untamed Africa. As near as he could judge, Eugene had pitched his tent in exactly the same place as Hemingway. He had also posed for a photograph in the same attitude. He had persuaded the Padre to photograph him against the rank wilderness of the vegetable garden, with Longonot in the background, a fine portrait to illustrate the dust cover of the book that would surely spring from his completed thesis. He had not yet decided what to call the book, which would be five hundred pages long, but was toying with *My African Experience* or *1001 Nights among the Masai*. The Padre had suggested *Elephant at the Pavilion End* – there had been one last cricket season, a fugitive from the Aberdares, followed by an assortment of interested natives who had never seen an elephant before – but Eugene had not been enthusiastic. 'Too frivolous,' he had insisted. 'You have to be more serious than that for the US market.'

His greatest hope, his single all-consuming wish, was that the Masai would before long make him a blood brother of the tribe. He had already written a blurb to this effect to go with the photograph in his book. Among the Masai it is a mark of high esteem to spit in another person's face, and Eugene had twice been spat upon already. Both occasions had been ecstatically recorded in his log, with a wealth of circumstantial detail. He was confident that if he continued to relate so successfully to the Masai, they would sooner or later come to accept him as one of their own.

'It's kind of a benediction,' he explained to the Padre. 'When the Masai spit in your face it means We see you. We accept you as a man like ourselves. We welcome you to our clan. They're giving me the tribe's blessing. But when they make me a blood brother, that's when I'll really know I'm one of them.'

'Nasty business, spitting.' The Padre did not care for it. 'They're all venereal, you know. I suppose really you just have to think of it as a blessing in disguise.'

'Pardon me?' said Eugene.

The syce was already at the door, in jodhpurs and dun-coloured tennis shoes, by the time the Padre had finished wording the advertisement for the new master. He showed it at once to Desmond:

Teacher of maths, algebra and geometry to CE standard. A sudden vacancy has occurred for a single male UK citizen under 55 to teach the above subjects and help with games. Experience not essential, but Service background an advantage.
Terms of contract: Two term contract, renewable if satisfactory. Free accommodation, return air fare to UK (if satisfactory).

Apply with CV and recent photograph to Major Gale, Haggard Hall, PO Box Naivasha, Kenya.

'I don't want to see their photographs,' said Desmond. 'Strike that bit out. It's far too depressing.'

'As you wish, headmaster.'

'And what about this Service background? It doesn't seem enough, somehow. We need to say something else as well. Something about the school being run along quasi-military lines.'

'Quasi-military lines?'

'Private school for boys run along quasi-military lines. It's important to get that bit in. That's what we're looking for, after all. A military type.'

The Padre revised the script.

'That'll do,' nodded Desmond. He sealed the envelope and handed it to the waiting syce. '*Kwenda* train. *Mara moja.*'

'*Ndio, bwana.*' Buckling his saddlebag, the syce mounted and turned his horse towards Naivasha. He set off down the track at a brisk canter. Behind him the school gates creaked shut and were locked into place with a wooden pole. Desmond and the Padre watched the dwindling figure until horse and rider had disappeared from view behind the fever trees.

'A military type, Padre. That's what we need.' Desmond was optimistic. 'Someone who's been around a while, who's seen a bit of action. Up the sharp end. That's all it takes to survive in a place like this. A man with character.'

6

About the same time as the syce reached Naivasha station, another train began a journey through the English countryside from London towards the British Army's Regular Commissions Board in Wiltshire. It carried a number of young men who, for one reason or another, were hoping to become an officer in the army. Among them was Martin Riddle.

The army takes three and a half days to assess potential officers, and for so long away from home Mrs Riddle had packed her son's case with more than usual care. She knew little about the Regular Commissions Board, but was determined to take no chances. She folded Martin's shirts for him – a clean one every day, a spare in case of accidents – and stacked them tidily in a neat pile. She did the same for his interview suit and anorak, and for half a dozen other things she thought he might need. She spent much of the morning thus employed and did not stop until only one small corner of his suitcase remained unfilled. Into this she slipped an apple for him to eat on the train.

'After all,' she told him, 'it's a long way to Westbury. You may not find anything else until you get there.'

From long habit Martin simply nodded politely. He was fond of his mother, but he wished sometimes that she would let him pack his own case. It was only fear of giving offence that prevented him from saying so.

'I expect the officers will invite you to have a drink with them,' Mr Riddle advised him as they walked to Purley Way station. 'If they do, ask for a sherry. Only one. And remember what I told you about saying Cheers when you drink it.'

'You will telephone, dear, won't you?' pleaded Mrs Riddle. 'As soon as you get in. We shall want to know you've arrived safely.'

'Yes mum. Of course I will.'

'You've got your ticket?'

'Yes mum.'

'And your travel money?'

Martin nodded.

'Well don't lose it.' Mrs Riddle gave Martin a hug. 'Here comes the train. Take care. And remember, whatever happens at the army, we'll always be proud of you. You know that. We always will. You're our boy.'

Whatever happens at the army. Munching his apple on the train, Martin could not help wondering just what *would* happen to him during the next three and a half days at the Commissions Board. In common with his mother, he knew almost nothing about the process of becoming an officer beyond what he had read in the advertisements and seen on TV. The Riddles were not a military family. Martin had decided to become a soldier more or less on the spur of the moment, a decision that still left him alternately horrified and elated at his own temerity. The Falklands War had been a major influence on his thinking, for he had not been immune to the outbreak of atavism that had swept the nation after the destruction of *HMS Sheffield*. He had followed the war closely on television from Darwin and Goose Green right through to the final surrender at Port Stanley. It was at Bluff Cove that he had first thought of becoming a soldier; at Tumbledown that he had decided to do something about it. Patriotism was his motive for joining up, what the army called the Falklands Factor as they sat gloomily through interviews with thousands of young men anxious to hurl themselves from aeroplanes. Patriotism, and the lack of teaching jobs in the area where his parents lived – for Martin was a teacher by aspiration; it was to the Royal Army Educational Corps that his aspirations were directed. To teach and be a soldier at the same time (so the promotional literature claimed) was to get the best of both worlds. This was the message that had brought him to Wiltshire.

A sergeant of the Guards met the train at Westbury. Martin had made a study of military uniform and recognised him from his buttons as a Coldstreamer.

'This way, gentlemen, please,' he said.

The candidates – there were forty-eight of them – followed meekly. They were driven by coach to the Board, which was situated in an old country house at the edge of the town. Once beautiful, the house had long ago been adapted to military requirements and was surrounded now by a cluster of specially erected outbuildings, each with a notice in front of it proclaiming its function – officers' mess, candidates' mess, candidates' spider (a sort of barrack room), lecture halls 1 and 2, interview rooms Alpha, Bravo, Charlie. Through the trees, a complicated assortment of poles, planks, pulleys, oil drums, scrambling nets and one inch ropes – each too short for its intended purpose – was visible outdoors on the Command Task area. These were the poles, planks and pulleys that featured so prominently in the advertisements. Candidates might sparkle in the lecture halls and at the written tests, but it was at the command tasks ('Transfer the heavy weight from A to B. Do not touch ground. Do not touch the crossbar. You must take the plank with you if you use it') that their suitability for the military life would ultimately be assessed.

In deep silence the candidates fell into line before the unseeing eyes of the permanent staff. There was something about the command tasks that unsettled even the best of them. The silence continued, intensified if anything, as they went forward in small groups to be issued with green denims and a large identification number to be worn over head and shoulders like a speedway rider. Then came documentation.

'Name?'

'Riddle.'

'Age last birthday?'

'Twenty-one.'

'Education?'

'Maths and physics at Brunel. A 2:2.'

The corporal looked up for the first time. 'I meant O levels. Have you got five O levels?'

'Of course.' Martin was taken aback. 'You have to, to get into Brunel.'

The corporal extended a hand. 'Certificate?'

'It's at home.' Martin fished in his pocket. 'I can show you my degree if you want it.'

'I dare say you can, mate, but it's the O levels I need. I've got to have the certificate.'

'I'll get my parents to send it.'

'No photocopies, mind. It has to be the real thing.'

Chastened, Martin rejoined the rest of his group. His O level certificate was in a glass frame on his bedroom wall. He wondered where he could find a telephone, and what his address was. The other members of the group, now he came to think of it, all had their certificates with them.

Martin was in Red Group. There were eight candidates in Red Group, each carefully selected according to type. There were two or three public schoolboys who stood on their own and compared cavalry regiments in loud voices; a pair of speechless grammar school youths in brown shoes; a slightly defensive REME corporal attempting officerhood for the second and last time; and a warlike little man from the Territorial Army, fierce in spectacles, whose every sentence on the coach had begun 'We were in this tank on Salisbury plain . . .' These were Martin's companions for the duration. Three quarters of them, according to a statistic cheerfully supplied by the supervising officer in his introductory talk, were certain to fail.

Martin's number in the group was Five. He learned this almost at once, when the sergeant in charge of the intelligence tests barked at him for picking up his pen before he had been told to. He learned it again during the first session on the assault course, when a moment's hesitation at the wrong end of a climbing rope earned him the rebuke 'Come on, Five, put more ginger into it,' from an officer standing behind him with a millboard. Officers with millboards, he soon discovered, were a universal feature of the place. They followed the candidates everywhere, watching, listening, probing, scribbling furiously whenever anything went wrong, writing nothing at all when things went right. It seemed to

Martin – who quickly began to dread the appearance of the board and the duck of the head that went with it – that the officers scribbled hardest whenever they came to him.

They even followed him indoors, the millboards, bringing the death wish to an otherwise unremarkable discussion group in which the eight candidates huddled together in a circle and talked about bull fighting, while the officers sat behind and marked them out of ten for logic, coherence and lucidity. The discussion, to say the least, was inhibited. Martin remained silent throughout, for he could think of nothing to say about bull fighting that was not banal or commonplace. It was not until the subject was switched to public schools – an essential topic for an educationalist – that he felt constrained to join in the debate.

The new discussion was opened by one of the public schoolboys, an elegant young man in a blue pinstripe suit. He had not been slow to promote the obvious view on bull fighting in the few minutes allotted to them. Nor was he slow now.

'I think they're a good thing,' he said. 'Public schools.'

'Why?' demanded the little man from the TA.

'For all sorts of reasons. Tradition, for one. Good education for another. You get a good education at a public school.'

'What about fagging and beating?'

'What about them?'

'Well, there's fagging and beating, isn't there? You can't say that's a good thing.'

'You can sometimes.'

'There's the Corps,' said another of the public schoolboys. Over lunch in the candidates' mess he had wanted everyone to know that he had been at Harrow. Now, in front of the officers, he was more reticent. 'The Corps's a good thing.'

'I doubt if it has much military value,' said the man from the TA.

'That's not the point. You don't join the Corps for military reasons. You join it so you can relax, get away from everything for a while. Do something . . .' he groped for the words ' . . . totally mindless. If you want to,' he added, sensing that this last bit had not gone down well with the millboards.

44

'Well it doesn't seem right to me,' said the TA man, seizing the advantage. 'I grant you there's a lot of good to be said about public schools, but there's a lot of bad too. On balance I wonder if the system is really valid any more.'

'Of course it is,' argued the first public schoolboy. 'It prepares you for life.'

'Does it? Does it really? All that fagging and beating?'

It was at this point that Martin plunged in. Though not a public school man himself, he knew all the literature and had long been fascinated by the phenomenon.

'We had the Corps at our school,' he announced.

The discussion flickered and died. Everyone turned politely to Martin and waited for him to continue. He opened his mouth to do so, but could think of nothing further to say. The death wish had suddenly come over him.

'That's as may be,' said the TA man in the silence that followed. He studied Martin malevolently. 'But the real point about public schools . . . .'

Martin heard no more. Writhing inwardly, he fiddled with his cuffs instead. The millboards were busy behind him. He felt that he had not scored highly on logic, coherence and lucidity.

He fared better next day on the planning project – a theoretical exercise involving the effective use of people, equipment, time and distance – for he was never happier than at a desk, a pen in his hand. The project was an individual one, no conferring, designed to seek out the imposters in the group, those whose verbal skills masked deeper, fundamental inadequacies. The candidates had ninety minutes to produce a solution. It seemed to Martin, eager to show his strength at last, that ninety minutes would be more than adequate.

'*The dead and the dying will have to be abandoned where they lie,*' he wrote, after half an hour's intense calculation. '*The wounded should be loaded aboard the camels and carried to hospital, leaving the women and children to guard the wreckage until help arrives.*'

He looked up at the clock. Fifty minutes to go. '*Or abandon the*

45

wreckage?' he wondered. *'Or abandon the women? Or abandon the wounded and carry the rest to the waterhole?'*

There was no real answer. The problem, he now realised, was insoluble. The aeroplane was of a secret design. It had crashed in the desert, a hospital in one direction, a waterhole in the other. With the scant resources at his disposal, there seemed little he could do about it.

'Or eat the camels? Or eat the women?' The only consolation was that no one else was enjoying the problem either. Glancing round, Martin was relieved to see indecision on every face – except of course for the TA man, who had already finished and with half an hour to spare was ostentatiously sitting back with nothing to do.

'The secret parts of the aeroplane will have to be loaded aboard the women,' Martin decided fifteen minutes later. *'Everyone else can walk to the waterhole, except for the seriously wounded who will proceed to hospital by camel.'* Then he crossed it out and put back what he had first thought of.

But it was the command task that Martin was to remember most vividly from his time at Westbury. The command task that took place on the last day, just before the candidates dispersed. He remembered it because the Major General himself, president of the Regular Commissions Board, came out of his office to watch. It was said that the Major General only came out to watch the borderline candidates, a piece of information that weighed heavily on Martin as he lined up the other seven and briefed them about the job in hand.

'Right,' he began. Everything in the army began with Right. 'The object of the exercise is to get this barrel,' he indicated a metal container filled with sand, 'over to there.' He indicated a tall wooden platform some twenty feet away, labelled inscrutably OFFLAG 223. 'We can use these two planks and that rope, but nothing and no one can touch the ground in between. Any questions?'

There were none. The problem, in theory at least, was straightforward. At Martin's command, three of the candidates slipped the rope around the longest plank and attempted to lower it onto

46

the nearest of several intermediate platforms, stepping stones to the objective, that lay in front of them. The plank proved to be six inches too short and rather too heavy. It wavered for a moment, then fell with a thud onto the forbidden ground below.

'That's a river there,' pointed out the supervising officer. 'With crocodiles in it.'

Martin tried again. Resisting an impulse to retrieve the plank himself, he ordered the TA man and the Old Harrovian to fish it out. Everyone else was still nursing his rope burns. Then he ordered the Harrovian to run up the plank and leap the remaining six inches to the platform.

'Why me?' demanded the Harrovian. 'Why not him? He's much smaller.'

'Because I said so.'

'But he's much lighter.'

'All right,' Martin told the TA man. 'You go.'

The TA man jumped onto the platform. The plank was passed up to him and he stood holding it aloft, like a victorious oarsman.

'Now what?' he asked nastily.

'Now we build a bridge.' It was Martin's plan to roll the barrel across a junction of two planks, into the waiting arms of the TA man. All went well until the middle. Then the planks gave way, depositing both TA man and barrel in the river again.

'There's high explosive in that barrel,' commented the supervising officer. The major general, a genial figure in gum boots, said nothing.

Twice more Martin attempted the crossing, the second time with success. Now the other candidates followed him onto the intermediate platform. They moved slowly, knowing time was short, anxious to increase their own chances of selection by destroying his. Eventually however, all eight had reached the rostrum and were clustered together in a space about three feet square.

'Remember the crocodiles,' thought Martin.

'Remember the crocodiles,' said the supervising officer.

Martin wished now that he had not ordered everyone onto the rostrum together. There was no room to turn round, let alone wield a plank efficiently. He wondered how he would deliver the barrel to the final objective, which was now an easy plank's length away. He was still wondering when time ran out and the supervising officer blew his whistle.

'Right,' he announced. 'Exercise ends. You can get down now.' Then 'Don't worry about it, Five. Three quarters of the candidates never make it in the time.'

Over his shoulder, the major general quietly consulted the millboard before drifting off to his office, accompanied by his dog. He had seen all he needed to. So had the officers. They put away their pencils and followed him in the direction of the mess. In their wake appeared ground staff, who ignored Martin and the others and began with tuneless whistles to reassemble the scattered equipment, ready for the next intake of candidates. Red Group, it could not have been plainer, was already dead. Long live Red Group.

7

That afternoon, after the last candidate had departed, the officers sat down with their millboards to decide who to recommend for training at Sandhurst. The discussion did not take long, for in most cases it was already obvious who was suitable and who not. They began with the little man from the Territorial Army. He had got on everyone's nerves and was top of the list for rejection.

'Dreadful fellow,' said the presiding brigadier. 'Did you see the way he combed his hair after the assault course?'

'*And* put his comb in his back pocket,' added the supervising officer.

The man from the TA was followed by the two grammar school youths and the REME corporal, who were returned respectively to the worlds of insurance, commerce and the corporals' mess. Two of the public schoolboys were accepted without demur; but the Old Harrovian was rejected, after some disagreement, on grounds of near-illiteracy. In less than an hour the officers went right through Red Group, bringing relief into two young men's lives, incalculable despair into five others. This left just Martin.

'There appears to be some doubt about his O levels,' reported the education officer. 'Odd really. He seemed perfectly intelligent to me.'

'Perfectly intelligent. But shy.' The supervising officer had noted Martin's cuff twiddling. 'He'd have to come out of his shell before he was any use to the army.'

'It says here he wants to join the education corps,' observed the brigadier in tones of mild incredulity.

'Nothing wrong with that,' the education officer said stiffly.

'All the same, I can't see him commanding a razor gang in the

49

Gorbals.' The brigadier was from a Scottish regiment. 'He'd be no bloody good up the sharp end if he couldn't.'

'He wouldn't be up the sharp end. He'd spend most of his time in the classroom.'

The brigadier was sceptical.

'I think we might take a chance,' suggested the education officer after a pause. 'They'll find him out at Sandhurst if we're wrong.'

'What do *you* think?' The brigadier turned to the supervising officer.

'I agree I can't see him sticking anybody with a bayonet.' The supervising officer was equivocal. 'He has no practical skills at all. He showed that on the assault course. But Sandhurst would brutalise him.'

'Anyway, we need educators. Otherwise you have to get them in from outside. And that means *civilians in the mess*.'

'I wonder,' said the brigadier. 'Really I do.' He studied Martin's photograph sadly. 'I suppose we'd better put it to the vote then. Who thinks he should be accepted for Sandhurst? I say no.'

'I say yes,' said the education officer.

'I say maybe,' said the supervising officer. 'On certain conditions only.'

'A split decision.' The brigadier wrote down the result. There was a procedure for split decisions. 'It will go to the major general. He has the final say. He saw Five in action, for what it was worth. Let him decide.'

8

It was already after four by the time Martin turned in the gate at
Purley Way. He had been hoping to arrive home unnoticed, but
Mrs Riddle was waiting for him in the hall.

'I failed,' he told her.

'What nonsense, Martin! Of course you didn't.' She gave him a
kiss. 'Don't be so silly.'

'I did.'

'How do you know?'

'I just know, that's all.'

'They'd never fail you. Of course they wouldn't. They'd have
more sense.'

'Yes they would. You don't know the army.'

'Nonsense, dear. I'm sure you did very well.' She helped him off
with his anorak. 'Don't let's talk about it now. I'll put the kettle
on and then you can tell me everything. It's jaffa cakes for tea.
Your favourite.'

Mrs Riddle busied herself in the kitchen. Normally she did not
make the tea until Mr Riddle got back from the office, but today
was special. 'Nearly ready,' she told Martin. 'As soon as the pot's
warm you can take a cup up to Gran.

'Now,' she said, when he returned. 'Tell me all about it. I want
to hear everything.'

Martin told her. He missed nothing out. How he had caught the
train, how he had arrived at Westbury, how the corporal had
wanted his O levels (Mrs Riddle had sent them off first class as
soon as he telephoned), how the sergeant had shouted at him for
picking up his pen. He told her about the assault course and
showed her a graze on his arm. He would have liked to have
shown her the planning project, so that she could see how difficult

51

it was, but the army had taken back the question papers at the end. So he got the group photograph out of his case and showed her that instead.

'Well,' she said, when he had finished. 'If that's how they treat you in the army, I'm not at all sure I want you to be a soldier. It doesn't sound very nice. I wonder if you shouldn't just go into ordinary teaching instead.'

'You know there aren't any jobs in ordinary teaching. I failed those three interviews.'

'Only because you were nervous.' She patted his knee. 'Something will turn up. Something always does. You'll see.'

'I just wish I could do the command task again. I know I could do better if I had another chance. I know I could.'

'You'll see.' Mrs Riddle unpacked Martin's dirty washing and took it through to the kitchen. 'I have a feeling everything will be all right in the end.'

'Yes mum, but it's now I'm worried about. If I don't get into the army I don't know what I shall do.'

'You'll get in.' Mrs Riddle had faith in her son. 'You remember that time in the scouts when you thought you'd failed your back-woodsman badge and Mr Gilpin had to come round to tell us you'd passed? That's what will happen now, I'm sure of it.' She emerged from the kitchen and put her arm around his shoulders. 'You're an awful silly to get so worked up. The army will accept you and everything will be fine. I know it will. Just you wait and see.'

Next morning, when Martin came down to breakfast, there was a buff envelope beside his plate with *On Her Majesty's Service* printed on it. The postmark was Westbury in Wiltshire.

Martin took a deep breath. This was it then. Watched by his mother and Gran, he tore the letter open.

'Well?' demanded Mrs Riddle.

Martin was too choked to speak.

'Come on, Martin. Tell us.'

'It's my expenses.' He waved a cheque. 'They're reimbursing my travel money.'

'Is that all?'

That was all. There was nothing else. Nothing about passing or failing, just an impersonal printed communication from a clerk in the pay office. Mrs Riddle snatched the letter from Martin and read it herself to make quite sure.

'Honestly,' she said. 'You'd think they'd be more considerate. Our poor Martin's waiting here and all they can do is give us all a fright.' She shook the letter at her mother. 'I say, Gran, they've given us a fright.'

'Quite right,' said Gran.

The next post was not until midday. Except for a trip to the shops to help his mother, Martin spent the rest of the morning in his room. Mr Riddle rang from the office at about eleven to find out what had been in the letter, and at great length Mrs Riddle told him. Martin lay on his bed, waiting for the postman to come, listening gloomily for the opening of the gate. He was determined whatever happened to get to the door before his mother. Towards midday he crept downstairs and took up a position beside the window, from where he could see two or three houses down the road in the direction of the post. His mother clattered in the kitchen, but Martin ignored her. He was not feeling communicative. He did not want sympathy yet. He wished, guiltily, that she would find something else to do.

When the postman did arrive, it was to deliver two letters. Both addressed to him, both *On Her Majesty's Service*. Martin opened the first at random:

The Board regrets that it is, at present, unable to recommend to the Ministry of Defence that you are a suitable candidate for entry to the Royal Military Academy, Sandhurst.

'I told you I'd failed,' he said.

'Let me see,' demanded Mrs Riddle. She came storming out of the kitchen. But Martin had turned his back.

The Board would, however, like to see you again in nine months' time, and the Vice President will write to you about this.

The other letter was from the brigadier, much against his

inclination, advising Martin to get in touch with the universities liaison officer at the Ministry of Defence.

'Why should you want to do that?' asked Mrs Riddle. 'I should think you've had enough of the army for a while. And what do they mean by deferred watch? It says here they've graded you deferred watch.'

'It means they want to have another look at me before they make up their minds.'

'Another look! Well really! I've never heard anything like it. Deferred watch indeed!'

Martin sat down. This was all too much, all at once. 'It means I've got to go through the whole business again,' he said moistly. 'Nine months from now.'

'If you still want to. Things might be different by then.' Mrs Riddle brightened up. 'Perhaps you'll have changed your mind about the army.'

'But what am I going to do in the mean time?'

'You can get a job. You can still teach.'

'I just don't know what to do.'

'Wait till Dad gets home. That's what.' Mrs Riddle was encouraging. 'You must talk it over with Dad. Talk to him. He'll know what to do.'

But Mr Riddle could offer little comfort. The army was outside his sphere of information. He read both letters over tea and shook his head.

'I don't know, son. It's up to you. I don't know what to suggest.'

'I must do something.'

'This what's-his-name man in London. Why don't you go and see him? See if he can tell you.'

'The universities liaison officer.'

'Go and speak to him. He must know what's going on. Take this letter and ask him what it's all about. That's what I'd do if I were you.'

'Well I think the whole thing's disgraceful,' said Mrs Riddle. And she went off to complain about it to Gran.

54

Two days later Martin reported to reception at the Ministry of Defence building in Berkeley Square. He was wearing his interview suit and had an appointment with the universities officer on the fifth floor.

He was escorted to the lift by a messenger in uniform, for strangers are not allowed to wander around the Ministry of Defence on their own. He had been issued with an official pass, recording his name, time of arrival, time of departure (left blank), and who he was going to see. The Ministry of Defence is a busy place, and a strong sense of atmosphere gripped Martin as he travelled upwards in the antiquated lift. It was exciting to think of the secrets the building must hold. The corridors on the fifth floor were full of people – cipher clerks, probably – all engaged on important work in the national interest. It seemed to Martin that behind every door messages were being beamed round the clock to British forces across the globe – troops in Hong Kong, aircraft in Belize, warships in the Indian Ocean or far below the ice caps of the North Pole. This was a building where decisions were taken, decisions of life or death. Here, in his humble way, Martin felt close to the centre of events.

The universities liaison officer (army) inhabited a small room overlooking the central courtyard. He was a retired colonel who had been at Cambridge in the days when anybody could get in. It was his job to recruit graduates and see to it that they obtained a commission with the minimum of fuss. He had Martin's file on his desk.

'Frankly they thought you were a bit wet,' he told him. 'You handled the written work all right, but you weren't so good in the field. Pretty feeble, in fact. That's where you slipped up.'

'I suppose you mean my command task?'

'That, and the assault course, and your approach in general. Not enough zing in it. The Board felt you could have done better.'

'More zing?'

'Your handling of the other candidates left a lot to be desired. You have to lead from the front in the army. That's what it's all about. It's no good sitting around waiting for others to take the

55

initiative. You've got to get out there and show them yourself. Grab them by the balls.'

Martin considered this. 'I suppose that's true,' he conceded. 'I should have grabbed them.'

'Between you and me you were a borderline case. The army needs graduates. It doesn't want them, but it needs them. You'd have passed first time if you'd put more zing into it.'

'Yes I see that now. But what can I do? It's a bit late, isn't it?'

'You can have another try in nine months. I suggest you use the time profitably.' This part of the universities officer's speech seldom varied. 'Find something to do for the next nine months that will help you to grow up.'

'What though?' Martin wanted to be told what to do. 'Have you any suggestions?'

'Ever been abroad?'

'We went to France once.'

'Go abroad. Get a job overseas somewhere. Get your knees brown. That's the sort of quality the army's looking for.'

A job overseas. Martin was alarmed. This was not what he had been expecting.

'I shall have to think it over,' he replied. His world tottered. He wondered how they would react in Purley Way. 'I'm not really . . . I've never. . . .'

'Go abroad,' said the universities officer firmly. 'Take the opportunity while you can, and get some practical experience of handling men while you're about it. That's my advice to you.'

—

So Martin looked for a job abroad. After consulting his parents he went to the public library near his home and spent a morning in the newspaper section, his mind full of possibilities. He would need a teaching job, of course, but where and how to find it?

The Riddles were a *Daily Telegraph* household and had been for as long as Martin could remember. But it was to the *Guardian* that he turned in his extremity. Although he did not really like the *Guardian*, or rather the people he saw reading it, he had to concede that its weekly education pages were the most comprehensive in

Fleet Street. There were plenty of jobs to choose from. More than he had ever imagined possible.

His eyes travelled down the list. Australia? He rejected Australia. Brazil? Teacher of maths and physics at the British school, Rio de Janeiro (must have three years' relevant experience at a recognised school). Cyprus? At least one year's experience for the Turk Maarif College, Nicosia. Dahomey, Mali, Zambia? All at least one year's experience, some as much as five. Indonesia, Nepal, the Solomon Islands? No experience necessary, but no interest in maths or physics either. Martin wondered if he dared apply for the geography job in the Solomons. He would have to find out where they were first.

Then he came to the Padre's advertisement.

9

'This Riddle's the only one then?'

'It appears so, headmaster. The response has not been encouraging.'

'Not exactly a military type.'

'Militarily inclined, though. And he knows about maths, which is what we're looking for.'

' "*If I am lucky enough to be accepted . . .* " I ask you, Padre. What kind of a letter is that?'

'An honest one. They so often aren't.'

'All the same though . . .'

'He can teach geometry, headmaster. That's all I ask.'

'You think I should take him on?'

'You must.' The Padre stood firm.

'Right you are, Padre. If you insist. But remember, this is your doing. Don't blame me if it doesn't work out.'

All week there had been packing in the Riddle household. All week, ever since Desmond's letter arrived, Mrs Riddle had been in a state.

'He's only allowed to take forty-four pounds with him,' she complained. 'That's one suitcase. How on earth can Martin take everything he needs in one suitcase? Can anyone tell me that?'

'He won't want many clothes,' Dad pointed out. 'It's very hot in the tropics.'

'But he'll need other things. You know he will. He can't possibly manage in one case. The airlines must be mad.'

'I went down to the surgery this morning,' said Dad. 'The doctor suggests a typhoid jab. And cholera.'

'And yellow fever. He may catch yellow fever.'

'And gamma globulin in case he gets hepatitis. Apparently it's quite common out there.'

'And polio. Mrs Simmonds at number fourteen, her nephew was in Nigeria. They get a lot of polio. And malaria. She says he ought to start taking the tablets at once.'

It was more than Mrs Riddle could bear. She sat down and dabbed her nose. 'I don't know,' she said, 'really I don't. Why Martin has to traipse off like this, in the middle of the jungle. Without even thinking about his parents. It's just not right. Really it isn't.'

'You mustn't worry yourself, pet.' Mr Riddle sought to console. 'You never know, it might be good for the lad. See a bit of the world, see how the other half lives. It's a marvellous opportunity for a young man. If I were his age . . .'

'He'll never get everything into one suitcase! I'm telling you, Graham! We're sending him halfway across the world, for goodness knows how long, with just the clothes he's standing up in.' She accepted a tissue. 'It's too much to put up with. Far too much. I honestly don't think I'll be able to cope.'

Yet she did cope – magnificently, as Mr Riddle said afterwards. When the chips were down, as he also said, she was splendid. She had never sent a son abroad before, but she swallowed her misgivings and rose honourably to the occasion.

Martin's clothes were her first concern. Mrs Riddle knew nothing about the uniform of an Englishman in the tropics, other than what common sense and Mrs Simmonds had told her. She remained undaunted. Armed with a list of Martin's measurements, she caught the London train and travelled to Piccadilly, to the tropical outfitters beside the Burlington Arcade. She had originally thought of taking Martin with her as well. But a prolonged session at the doctor's had left him in bed with cholera, and perhaps also typhoid. So she travelled alone.

When she returned that evening she was carrying two bushjackets, two pairs of khaki trousers – long, no trouble with snakes – seven pairs of cotton socks, two pairs of lightweight pyjamas, a pair of veldschoen, a set of green aertex underwear and a khaki bush hat, buttoned up on one side and circled with a ribbon of fake leopardskin.

'It looks nice on you,' she said, adjusting the hat for him. 'It's just what they wear in Africa.'

Martin studied the mirror dubiously. 'Are you sure? I wonder if it isn't a bit . . . you know.'

'Nonsense, dear. Everyone wears them. It's to do with the heat.'

Martin did not argue. He was still feeling feverish. In any case the events of the past few days, crowding thick and fast upon him, had deprived him of the will to resist. His world had been turned upside down by Desmond's letter. He was still unsure how to react.

All he knew for certain was that he was being rushed. He had felt it that first day when the letter dropped onto the mat, complete with airline ticket and date – almost immediate – for his departure. He had felt it again when Mrs Riddle took him to the doctor. Now, in bushjacket, veldschoen and leopardskin hat, he felt it once more.

Nor was this all, for Martin had another preoccupation. He had just received a second letter from Kenya. A letter, mildly puzzling, from the Padre:

Dear Mr Riddle,

I gather from Major Gale that you will shortly be joining us at Haggard Hall. May I say how pleased I am to hear it? We are an isolated little community here and we always welcome new faces. I am sure you will enjoy your time with us.

I wonder if I could ask you a special favour? I have ordered a pair of Syrian Dewlaps (squabs) from a man in London – very reliable chap, I always deal with him – and I was wondering, since you are coming out anyway, if you wouldn't mind bringing them with you? They would have to travel as hand luggage, of course, but I would be very much easier in my mind if I knew they were with someone, rather than just travelling as cargo. You never know what happens to cargo. They wouldn't need much attention on the journey, just a little air and water, and some corn. They'd be no trouble.

60

PS. Stands Jackson's of Piccadilly where it did? If so, do you think it would be possible to buy me a dozen jars of Patum Peperium — Gentleman's Relish — from the delicatessen department? You can't get it out here. I would reimburse you, of course.

It was a puzzling letter, but easily resolved. A telephone call to the man named by the Padre identified the Dewlaps as racing pigeons. As soon as he was better, Martin went to collect them. He found them in a cardboard box, neatly tied up with string.

'They're good birds,' said their owner, an unshaven individual in an overcoat. 'Bred 'em myself. Keep them full of vitamins, see they get plenty of yeast, you'll be all right.'

The birds struggled to retain their footing as Martin retraced his steps to the Underground. They sat beside him, grumbling occasionally, all the way to Green Park. Here he discovered that Jackson's of Piccadilly no longer existed. After some hesitation he went instead to Fortnum and Mason's, just along the street, and bought a dozen pots of Patum Peperium from the tail-coated assistant behind the front counter. The price for twelve pots seemed to him exorbitant. He was glad someone else was paying.

Thus equipped, he prepared for his journey to Africa. His suitcase, packed and repacked several times, was lugged into the bathroom and placed on the scales. It registered forty-eight pounds. Against all her instincts Mrs Riddle withdrew a bushjacket, a pair of desert boots, and a bottle of insect repellent. The case weighed forty-five pounds. She withdrew a mosquito net and six of the pots of Gentleman's Relish and wrapped them all up in a plastic carrier bag from Sainsbury's. They would have to travel as hand baggage, she decided, alongside the pigeons.

Martin's flight was due to leave from Gatwick. All the Riddles travelled down on the train. The Sussex fields as they passed were alive with the colours of autumn, the splendid colours of the English countryside at its best. Martin felt somehow as if he was seeing them for the last time. His emotions, as he checked in his baggage, were decidedly mixed. A blend of horror and elation, the same blend that had prompted him to join the army, now assailed him again. He was terrified to be going to Africa, but he was also glad. He did not know why, but he was glad.

'You've got your passport?' asked Mrs Riddle. 'And your medical certificates?'

'Yes mum.'

'Make sure you always keep your passport with you. You never know when you may need it.'

'All right.' Martin was nervous. Looking about him, it was impossible to tell which of the passengers at the door of the departure lounge would be journeying with him to East Africa. What was certain though was that no one else was wearing a bushjacket or a hat with a leopardskin band.

'You will write? As soon as you get there? Tell us what it's like?' Martin nodded.

His flight was called. As one, the Riddle family shot to their feet.

'Quickly, Martin. You don't want to miss it.'

'Goodbye mum.

'Goodbye dad.

'Goodbye gran.'

Martin picked up the Sainsbury's bag and the pigeons. They were awkward to hold together. In his other hand he carried his passport. He joined the queue for the departure lounge. The passport officer looked at his picture and nodded him through. Martin turned, waved gravely at his family, and was gone.

'He's on his own now,' said Dad.

10

The flight to Nairobi lasted nine hours, including a stop at Frankfurt to take on more passengers. For Martin, strapped to his seat in the rear cabin, this was the first time he had had to himself since the day Desmond's letter arrived.

He was relieved, after a fashion, now that the expedition had got off the ground at last. The tension of the past few days, the uncertainties about his future, the continual harassment from his mother – all were safely behind him, and although there was still much to come that he did not care to think about, he suspected that the worst must be over. His spirits lifted with the aeroplane. Now that he had come to terms with the idea, he was pleased to be going abroad; pleased also to have a job, with the guarantee of two terms' employment and a return flight at the end. The truth is that he was keen to become a schoolmaster at any price, even in Africa. He felt that teaching, whether of small boys or soldiers, was the only vocation for which he had any aptitude.

To get into the right mood for the journey, he had gone to the library before he left and taken out several well-known books about Kenya – *Born Free, Out of Africa*, the *Kenya Diary* of Richard Meinertzhagen. These, together with the televised version of *The Flame Trees of Thika*, provided much background information about his new environment. He had also stumbled across a popular history of the English in Kenya, which he had gone out and bought. He read it now on the plane. It turned out to be an entertaining story of lords and ladies, drug addicts and pioneers, adulterers and black sheep; a story of high altitude eccentricity, informally told, in which everyone drank or fornicated or was sent Home in disgrace. Martin read it with pleasure, but also with mild alarm. How, he wondered, would he ever fit in to such a society?

He had reached Chapter Seven, the point where Evelyn Waugh's friend Raymond de Trafford seduces two settler women in one night, when the German passengers came on board. They were holiday makers, industrial workers from the Ruhr en route for a month in the sun. They made a great deal of noise as they found their seats, but Martin was happy to see them, for among the Agfas and Instamatics that brushed past him he recognised at least two bush hats similar to his own. This gave him a confidence he had hitherto lacked, since he did not like to be alone in wearing a leopardskin hatband. He preferred the solidarity of numbers.

The seat next to Martin was vacant. It was claimed by a tall bearded German carrying a cine camera in a black holdall. He attempted to stow the camera in the rack above Martin's head, only to discover that the space was already occupied by the Padre's pigeons. From the expression on his face it was evident that the German had not been expecting to find pigeons there.

They were in a cardboard box, the same box, slightly ill smelling, in which Martin had collected them from their previous owner. Although too young to fly, the squabs were beginning to resent their confinement in such a small space. They voiced their resentment in long, sullen bombilations which competed disconcertingly with the noise of the aero engines. From time to time, increasingly as the flight wore on, Martin visited them with ministrations of corn and water. Whenever he did, they fought viciously with each other in a vain attempt to escape. They were unattractive creatures, thin and featherless, devoid of adult grace. They blinked reproachfully at Martin and fouled themselves – a reproach that was mutual, for Martin resented the obligations they laid upon him. Between Martin and his charges, the atmosphere was not cordial.

Before long, to his alarm, the birds began to lose heart. First one, then the other sank listlessly into a stupor from which nothing would rouse them. They seemed oblivious to their surroundings – as if beyond caring. They took no further interest in the world and what it had to offer, but simply squatted gloomily and held their own counsel.

'*Vögel, ja?*' asked the German, who liked to get things straight.

'*Ja, vögel,*' Martin confirmed. He peered at them through the air holes in the lid. They were hunched down among their own shoulderblades, showing few signs of life. They did not seem happy. 'As long as they don't die on me, that's all.'

They did die. Somewhere over Lake Turkana, so far as Martin could judge. Mount Kenya was below the port wing tip, heavy with snow, when he made the discovery. The squabs had toppled over and were lying motionless in a pool of saturated cardboard, their corn untouched, their wings folded in death. There was nothing Martin could do for them.

This was a blow, for it meant that he had been put to considerable inconvenience to no avail. It also meant, so far as his first meeting with the Padre was concerned, that he would be beginning his new career on a sour note.

'Tot,' observed the German. 'Alles tot.'

Thus it was that Martin's first impression of Kenya, of the African continent, was not the usual one of Jomo Kenyatta airport, flat and featureless on a rain-sodden morning; nor even of Mount Kilimanjaro, a hundred miles away above the cloud. He thought only of the two limp carcasses and of what he was going to do about them. His initial instinct, as the plane came in to land, was to deposit the birds in a litter bin and have done with it. But then he wondered about the Padre. The Padre might not accept his explanation. Better perhaps to produce the corpses intact, as it were, as evidence of his good faith. If he played his hand right, he could even feign surprise when the Padre opened the box.

With this in mind, Martin gathered together the birds and his Sainsbury's bag and joined the queue for the exit. He did not have the birds on his conscience, he told himself; it was not his fault that they had died. Not even a pigeon lover could have saved them.

The queue for the exit was headed by the Germans. In one seething mass, desperate not to lose sight of each other, they clattered down the steps and across to the terminal building. It was early morning in Nairobi, surprisingly cold, and the passport officials had not yet woken up to the day. They stamped passports at a leisurely African pace. One by one the Germans fought through and advanced to the carousel to reclaim their baggage. Here, long before the first suitcase appeared, they were rejoined by Martin and the rest of the passengers. Then came customs.

Martin's case passed without comment, as did the pots of Gentleman's Relish. But the cardboard box was a different matter. The customs officers at Nairobi were the sort of men who become suspicious if someone tries to bring dead birds into a country. They took one look inside the box, then at each other, then at Martin.

'Why are you bringing these into Kenya?'

Martin told them.

The customs men were not convinced. They put their heads together and conferred in a foreign tongue – Martin guessed Swahili. A senior customs man was summoned. He eyed Martin speculatively as the others took one corpse each and searched it for drugs, holding it up to the light and probing every orifice for signs of unnatural entry. Nothing was found, but the officers remained suspicious. What, they asked themselves, was Martin's game?

'May I go now?' he inquired.

'You are sure you have nothing to declare?'

'Quite sure.'

The customs men were unhappy, but there was little they could do.

'*Ndio*, you may go.' Reluctantly they gave him back the birds. 'Welcome to Kenya.'

All three watched as Martin plunged into the melée around the door of the arrivals hall. He did not look back. He was worried about his suitcase, which had been snatched from him by a porter who was busily trying to steer him towards a taxi driven by his uncle. Martin was not used to having his luggage carried. Nor did he wish to take a taxi. He wished to take the airport bus into Nairobi, and thence to the railway station, where he would catch the train to Naivasha. These were his instructions from Desmond.

'You take a taxi,' said the porter. 'Very good taxi.'

'I don't want a taxi. I want the bus.'

'You take a taxi. Bus no good. Bus *bure*.'

'I don't want a taxi.'

'Bus not running today. *Kwisha kwenda.*'

'Look, please don't argue. Just take me to the bus stop.'

'Taxi. . . .'

'Bus. . . .'

The taxi dropped Martin at the station. On the way the porter's uncle persuaded him to part with a sizeable sum of English money in return for Kenyan currency at twice the official rate of exchange. Martin's pockets were filled with shillings and cents, the fruits of a transaction that would have landed him in prison if it had ever come to light.

He saw little of Nairobi during the journey, for the railway station was on the wrong side of town. There had been a time in the not too distant past when travellers from the airport ran a very real risk of colliding with a zebra or wildebeest on the road; but the growth of industrial estates along the route had changed all that. Factories, wire fences and notice boards proclaiming such and such a company's confidence in the future of Kenya were all that Martin could see, and behind them a skyline dominated by the high-rise glass and concrete of the Kenyatta Centre. Nairobi's game park, one of the wonders of the world, was to his left – but from the road there were no animals in sight, not even a distant giraffe. Nothing of tooth and claw was visible between him and a rather dull horizon. This was scarcely Africa as Martin had expected it; the television at home had painted an entirely different picture. He wondered if he was going to be disappointed in his new life.

Another of the taxi driver's nephews tried to seize his suitcase outside the station, but this time Martin was too quick for him. He clung firmly to his own possessions and found his way unaided to the booking office.

'How much is a single ticket to Naivasha?'

'One hundred and thirty-five shillings.'

Martin collected his ticket and moved away. Soon he was back.

'It says ninety-five on that board.'

'I am sorry, my friend. A mistake.'

Martin pocketed his refund and moved off again. The train was due to leave in twenty minutes, which gave him just enough time to write a postcard to his parents, recording his safe arrival. He wavered between a photograph of an elephant or a Giriama maiden with bare breasts, and settled finally for the elephant. '*Arrived safely*,' he wrote. '*All well*.' Then he boarded the train.

There were no other white men in the compartment; most Europeans travelled up-country by car. Martin's only companions were an elderly Sikh in a turban and an African couple who fell silent as soon as he entered and looked at him with undisguised curiosity. The pallor of his skin marked him out as a newcomer to the country, as did the bush hat and supermarket bag. The Africans studied him from top to toe. Whatever next? they wondered privately.

Martin's seat was by the window. For the first twenty miles or so the journey through Kikuyuland confirmed his initial disillusion at his new surroundings. The view from the window was endlessly the same – goats, huts, banana patches, goats, huts, maize plantations – a scene of rural desolation infinitely tedious to the eye. Wherever natives lived in large numbers, as he later discovered, there the earth lost its beauty. Wherever two or three huts were gathered together, there the grass withered, the corn husks rotted, the water lay foul and stagnant. There was no charm in Kikuyuland; none that he could discern.

Later the view improved. It was getting towards lunch time, and the early morning rain clouds over Nairobi had given way to bright sunshine, African sunshine, dominant in a sky that somehow seemed higher and more blue than in England. The landscape altered too, for the train had completed the crossing of Kikuyuland and was approaching the escarpment at the edge of the Rift Valley. Without warning the earth gave way and fell two thousand feet to the floor below. Martin was suddenly conscious of a limitless horizon, of cloud shadows far beneath him, of sunlight glittering on a distant lake; of a depth and scale and sweep to the land that he had never before contemplated. 'Breathtaking' was the word the guidebooks used for the Rift Valley; Martin did not dispute it. A valley so large that it dwarfed Mount Longonot, nine thousand feet above sea level, and other volcanoes as well. A valley prominent on satellite photographs, stretching half the length of Africa. A fault in the earth's crust, according to the geography lessons at Haggard Hall, but a fault like no other Martin had ever seen.

His companions were less impressed by the spectacle. They remained in their seats, stolidly immune to their heritage, as the train descended by degrees to the floor of the rift. It was approaching Naivasha, through territory that had formerly belonged to the Masai. Not far away was the site of the Kedong massacre, where six hundred and fifty skulls had once littered the ground in an argument over a girl. There were few warriors about now, for the land had long ago been settled by the British. Most of the wild life had gone too, although small herds of impala or Thomson's gazelle were occasionally visible through the scrub. Thomson himself had passed this way on his expedition towards Lake Victoria. The impression of Mount Longonot that he had recorded then, graphically reworked by Rider Haggard, was the impression that confronted Martin now: a remote and mysterious volcano, rising sharply out of the plain, its bowl so many miles across as to support a complete life system with never any knowledge of the larger world outside. A remote and mysterious volcano, and beside it a savagely beautiful lake. Beside them both the railway line, straddled by a tin-roofed cluster of dwellings that marked the one-street township of Naivasha.

There had been nothing at Naivasha before the coming of the railway. There was not much there now. As the train drew in, Martin caught a glimpse of perhaps a dozen native shops and a small beer hall, stained with age. That was all. The post office, the telephone exchange and the police station were obscured by fever trees; the petrol pump too. Naivasha had once been a jumping off point for the surrounding European farms, but it had never attracted the commerce of other, similar places along the line. It had simply remained what it had always been – a jumping off point.

Martin retrieved his luggage from the rack and opened the carriage door. He was the only passenger to alight. Something of the thrill of the pioneer came over him as he did so, for bold men had passed this way before – men with bullet loops in their coats. In their footsteps he had travelled to what was plainly one of the ends of the earth, a cause, if not for congratulation, then at least for quiet jubilation.

Major Gale had arranged to collect him from the train. Suitcase in one hand, Sainsbury's bag and pigeons in the other, Martin stepped expectantly towards the barrier.

Thus his new life began.

11

It began not quite as he had expected, because Desmond was not there to meet him. There were no white men on the platform, none outside the station, none anywhere. Martin was alone.

He waited three quarters of an hour, hoping the headmaster would turn up, before he started to panic. To be on his own in a strange and hostile environment was the very nightmare Martin had always dreaded. But it was a nightmare that would have to be faced. He patted the pocket where he kept his passport and urged himself to keep calm.

'I want to ring Haggard Hall,' he told the stationmaster. 'Where can I find a telephone?'

'No telephone to Haggard Hall.'

'Is there a bus?'

'No bus.'

'Taxi then?'

'No taxi.' The word meant nothing to the stationmaster. He was a cheerful Kikuyu with a gap in his teeth, anxious to help.

'Well how does one get to Haggard Hall?'

'You have no car?'

'No. I came on the train.'

'Is better if you have a car.'

'But I haven't. I came on the train.'

There was truth in this. The stationmaster ruminated for a while, then pointed with his chin. 'Is that way,' he said.

'How far?'

'Not far.' Not far was an African unit of measurement, meaning anything between five and a hundred miles.

So Martin set out to walk. There was nothing else for it. He hoisted his luggage and headed off in the direction indicated by

71

the stationmaster. He would have preferred to deposit his bags in the left luggage office, to be retrieved at a later date, but there was no left luggage office at Naivasha. It was not that sort of station.

In a few minutes he had cleared the town and was walking along a dusty murram road, shielded from the sun by a grove of yellow-boled umbrella trees, interspersed here and there with jacaranda. The plain on either side was green and lavish, far removed from the sere brown aridity that Martin had hitherto associated with Africa. There were no human beings in sight, nor any habitation. The lake was a vigorous blue, reflecting the sky, and feathered around the edges with clumps of papyrus and water lily. It was a graceful scene – beautiful even. In less trying circumstances, Martin might have recognised it as idyllic.

Ahead of him a secretary bird dashed quizzically onto the track and kept him company for perhaps fifty yards before veering off again. It was followed by a flock of guinea fowl which ran straight across in a state of high alarm. There were vervet monkeys in the trees and water buck among the bougainvillea. A herd of Thomson's gazelle came to look at him, then made off at speed, wagging their tails behind them. The plain was alive with animals – not the giant carnivores and herbivores of the travel brochures, but the gentler creatures of the grasslands, tamer in habit and more pastoral.

Martin was pleased. This was more like the Africa of the films. He did not know it, but the greater part of *Living Free* had been filmed around the lake – Elsa the lioness lay buried on Crescent Island, not far from his destination. A number of Tarzan films had been made there too, usually in the papyrus swamp a few hundred yards from one or other of the lakeside hotels that catered periodically for foreign film crews. Naivasha had known its fair share of stars over the years; Clark Gable, who never queried his lines, had once identified it authoritatively as gorilla country.

Martin pressed on. He had walked several miles and his suitcase was beginning to weigh heavily. He was also suffering from jet lag. Yet his spirits were not low, for he was slowly coming to appreciate the wisdom of the army's universities officer in consigning him to this delightful spot. It was all so different to what he had expected.

Even the air was different. There was a freshness to it, a high altitude sparkle that was novel to him, that made his blood fizz. He felt light headed.

Presently a soft breeze arose, ruffling the waters of the lake into sudden paroxysms of sapphire. The grass waved and the trees rustled. A turtle dove cooed distantly, breaking the otherwise total silence of midday. Towards evening the plain would come to life again, would pulsate with the horrors of sudden, savage death; but for the moment it was wholly at peace with itself. The hawk had sheathed its talons, the dik dik lay down with the viper, the leopard rolled over on its back and dozed. Animals basked everywhere. The world was in repose.

Into this Arcady, without warning, there intruded a harsh, alien sound.

In fact Martin had been vaguely aware of it for some time, the far off sound of hounds baying, as if in pursuit of a quarry. There was also a sharper, more metallic sound – difficult to identify – that echoed intermittently from the bush somewhere to his left. In England he might have identified it as a hunting horn; here he could not be so sure.

He wondered how much further it was to Haggard Hall. He was looking forward to arriving, not least because the prospectus made it sound an intriguing place. Martin had consulted the *Public and Preparatory Schools Yearbook* before leaving England, and the entry on Haggard Hall had been oddly cryptic: *Facilities include an airstrip, shooting range and riding stable under a fully qualified instructress. Emphasis is placed on character, discipline and good manners. There is a matron.* Martin's own education had never taken him more than a few hundred yards from Purley Way, but he had read countless books about English boarding schools and was familiar with the ethos. It was an admirable system, that had produced many famous men. Bunter, Stalky, the Fourth of June – Martin was determined to enjoy the same experience, if only at second hand.

The hounds bayed again, closer now. The sound seemed to be coming from behind a ridge of high ground overlooking the lake. Along the top of the ridge, about half a mile away, a group of

Africans suddenly came into view, heading towards Martin at a brisk trot. There were a dozen of them and they carried spears.

Martin looked round. The plain was deserted except for him. He began to feel uneasy.

The horn was closer too, definitely a horn.

Martin put down his suitcase. This was all very peculiar. Not what he had been led to expect. He wished he had waited longer for Major Gale to pick him up at the station.

A light aircraft swept overhead, so low that Martin could see the pilot's face and the words *Kenya Police* on the fuselage. The pilot circled twice around him and spoke urgently into his headset.

Martin picked up his suitcase again and hurried on. He did not know what else to do. Clearly events were about to unfold on the plain; equally clearly, these events had nothing to do with him. He wondered perhaps if there was a killer elephant loose.

He had not got much further on when a small figure broke cover ahead of him and scuttled across the road into the safety of the bushes the other side. It moved so fast that Martin barely got a glimpse of a white boy, about twelve years old, before it was gone.

It was followed, after a lengthy interval, by a Landrover which came towards Martin at great speed. He was relieved to see that the driver was a distinguished-looking white man in a tweed coat.

'You seen Smith-Baggot anywhere? A small boy with a gun.'

'I think so. He went that way.'

'Thanks.' The driver let out the clutch and drove on another thirty yards before stopping again. Dust was still falling on Martin in a golden haze as the driver reversed alongside him.

'Who are you anyway?'

'Martin Riddle. I'm a teacher at Haggard Hall.'

'Christ,' said Desmond. Then, 'Well hop in. I'd better give you a lift.'

Martin hopped in. His suitcase, pigeons and Sainsbury's bag were somehow absorbed into the back of the Landrover, which was already full of African spearmen. The front seat was vacated for him by an elderly Ndorobo with perforated ear lobes, who went to sit on the bonnet instead.

'My tracker,' Desmond explained. 'Smith-Baggot ran away this morning. We've got to get him back before he reaches the mountains.'

He glanced at Martin's hat in disbelief and let out the clutch again. Martin held on with both hands as the Landrover plunged off the road without warning and accelerated through the bush towards the Aberdares. The tracker clung to the bonnet, looking ahead for signs of their quarry.

'First time in Africa?' asked Desmond.

Martin nodded.

'It isn't like England, you know. If a boy runs away here, anything could happen. Anything at all. That's why we have to get Smith-Baggot back.'

Martin nodded.

'We had something like this happen once before actually. Before my time, thank God. A boy named Armstrong.' Desmond swerved. 'He ran away and was never seen again. During the Emergency it was, when there was a shortage of manpower. They never even found the bones.'

'You think he was eaten?'

'Probably. If the game didn't get him, the nigs must have done. Or the heat. Either way, he disappeared without trace. When you get to school, you'll come across the Armstrong Memorial Cup in the dining hall. That's all that's left of him. It was the least the school could do.'

Martin digested this in silence. Desmond drove on, sometimes at speed, sometimes at a walking pace as the old Ndorobo studied the terrain ahead. Presently they bumped across a dry river bed and came upon a group of figures huddled together in conference. It consisted of the dozen spearmen Martin had seen earlier, a radio operator, a police sergeant with a tracker dog, and a stout European lady on a horse.

'Any luck?' Desmond asked the stout lady.

'Not a thing. I thought we had him, but the hounds went cold.' She indicated a pair of foxhounds who were circling the police dog warily. 'I gave them Smith-Baggot's games shorts, but they lost the scent.'

'What about the spotter?'

'Nothing.' She shielded her eyes in search of the plane. 'He's covered everywhere between here and Naivasha. He wants to know if he's to go on trying.'

'I should think so,' said Desmond. 'For the moment at least.'

'The bill will be enormous.'

'I shall send it to the Smith-Baggots. They can afford it.'

Martin studied the lady on the horse. He had had some idea that European women in the tropics spoke with a colonial accent, but this one held forth in tones of fruitiest Belgravia. She was about sixty, slightly unkempt, dressed in riding boots, a skirt and a shapeless *terai* hat. She carried a hunting horn and a whip. When she spoke, the foxhounds slunk closer to the ground – as indeed did the police sergeant and the spearmen.

'He's around here somewhere,' said Desmond. 'He's been seen. He can't have gone far.'

'If he's heading for home, he'll have to take the national park track over the Aberdares. That's the place to catch him.'

'I'll get up there with the Landrover,' Desmond told her. 'You take your boys and fan out behind us. He'll have to break cover sooner or later. See if you can't flush him out.'

It had been raining in the Aberdares that morning, and for five days previously. A wooden '*Park closed*' sign across the track indicated that it had been washed away in several places.

'To hell with that,' said Desmond, nosing past it.

When would all this travelling stop, Martin wondered, as the vehicle slithered ambitiously uphill. By now he should have been safely at Haggard Hall, sleeping off the effects of his journey. Instead he was illegally climbing a mountain, in the company of people he had never met before – most of them carrying spears – in pursuit of a child he didn't know. Gatwick, Frankfurt, Nairobi, Naivasha, the Aberdares, when would it all end?

They were approaching eight thousand feet before Desmond called a halt. They had reached a spur of the mountains overlooking the plains below – a good vantage point for keeping Smith-Baggot's approach route under surveillance.

'We'll split up,' Desmond told Martin. 'You take Mogadishu,' he indicated a spearman with a fearsome gash across his face where his nose should have been. 'I'll take the other boys. We'll comb the forest either side of the track. See what we can turn up.'

'Right,' said Martin without much confidence.

'You'll need these.' Desmond gave him a pair of binoculars. 'And this.' He handed over a rifle. 'It's a .270. A Rigby. There are five rounds in the clip. Should be enough.'

'Right,' said Martin with even less confidence. This was not the moment to confess that he had never held a rifle before.

He set off uncertainly through the forest. Mogadishu followed one pace behind, carrying his spear across his chest. In private life he was head groundsman at Haggard Hall, with particular responsibility for rolling the cricket pitch. He was still wearing his working clothes.

The route led downhill across a meadow flushed with rain. Martin skirted the edge and entered a grove of yellow-headed cassia, so thick that he could not see more than a few yards. He moved cautiously, not knowing what to expect. Mogadishu took his cue from Martin, proceeding stealthily out of politeness to the white bwana in the funny hat. The undergrowth barely rippled with their passing; progress was uniformly slow. Once, they disturbed a family of forest hog, which trotted off with tails at the high port; once a lone hyena, indignant at the intrusion; once a pile of old droppings, scuffed to pieces across their path.

'*Kifaru*,' said Mogadishu. 'Rhino.'

'Rhino? Here?'

'Not now, bwana. Gone.'

Impressed, Martin gripped his rifle more firmly. He wondered privately how it worked. He was far too shy to ask for instruction.

He crawled up a small incline and raised his binoculars, searching the lower reaches of the valley for signs of movement. Far below, the police spotter plane probed the reverse slopes on the same errand. The sun was still powerful, but the shadows across the land were beginning to lengthen. In a short while the African night would descend with all the abruptness of the tropics. If Smith-Baggot was to be recaptured, it would have to be soon.

77

'There's no sign of him,' reported Martin, wriggling down again. 'Not that I can see.'

'We go back?' suggested Mogadishu. 'Tell Bwana Gale.'

Martin led the way back to the Landrover. He was feeling more confident now, more relaxed. Almost abreast of the situation. The binoculars were a help, thumping reassuringly against his chest. They made him look the part.

Pushing into a clearing, he came upon a Cape buffalo grazing peacefully a few yards away. It was a fine-looking beast, not much larger than a cow. Martin stopped to admire it. The buffalo took no notice of him, but turned its back and continued to graze.

'I wish I had a camera,' he said.

There was no answer. Looking round, Martin saw Mogadishu peering at him from behind a podo tree some fifty yards distant. He had a hand on the trunk, ready to shin up it at a moment's notice.

Martin walked on. Mogadishu rejoined him circuitously, taking care not to upset the buffalo. They reached the track slightly uphill and found their way down to the vehicle.

'No joy,' said Desmond. 'Can't find the bugger anywhere.'

'What happens now?'

'Who knows? We shall have to get back to school. We can't stay up here in the dark. Smith-Baggot will just have to fend for himself.' Desmond admitted defeat. 'It's for the police now – and his parents will have to be told. A damn nuisance, frankly.'

He slammed the car door and started the engine. Mogadishu and the others scrambled into the back. Martin took his place in the passenger seat. The Landrover slipped into gear and lurched unsteadily downhill, skittering from side to side over an often non-existent track. Soon night would fall. On impulse, as the light began to fade, Martin took off his bush hat and threw it out of the window.

12

It was wholly dark by the time they reached Haggard Hall. At first glance the school was best observed from afar, framed in its natural setting of mountain and lake. It was also impressive at close quarters – an array of leaded lights, stone mullions and morning glory under a red-tiled gable. But Martin saw none of this in the gloom. He saw only a fence of barbed wire picked out in the headlights, and an overcoated night watchman waiting sombrely for them at the gate.

Desmond led the way indoors. He went straight to the dining hall, where the boys had assembled after supper. Some seventy or eighty rose politely as he entered. They were illumined by a single electric bulb from the generator, dressed alike in the school uniform of khaki shirts and shorts. The older ones sat at the back, the eight and nine-year-olds in front. They viewed Desmond's arrival with a blanket expression of guilt and mistrust, tinged this evening with a low frisson of expectancy.

'We won't mention Smith-Baggot,' Desmond told Martin. 'No good giving them the wrong end of the stick. Not until we know what's happened to him.'

It was film night at Haggard Hall, the one night of the week when there was no prep. An ancient projector stood ready at one end of the room; a white sheet at the other, draped across the bay window to provide a screen.

Desmond stood in front of the sheet. 'There's been a slight change of programme,' he informed the boys. 'We were going to show you a film about the Dutch herring fleet tonight, followed, I think, by rather an interesting one about Venezuela's fight against malaria. But the syce wasn't able to get to the station today to pick up the film, so we're having something else instead. You'll be glad to hear that Lady Bullivant has kindly offered, at *very* short notice, to let us see once again the films of her early life in India.'

The applause that greeted this announcement was prolonged and genuine. It had been a day of great excitement at the Hall. Smith-Baggot's escape, a feat without living precedent, had put new heart into the boys. They were in excellent mood. They had seen Smith-Baggot's shorts taken away and fed to the dogs; they had seen men with guns search the grounds; they had seen an aircraft land on the playing fields. They knew that whatever happened to Smith-Baggot was bound to be awful. Lady Bullivant's memoirs, in the circumstances, would round off a perfect day.

Lady Bullivant was the riding mistress. Martin recognised her at once as the stout lady on the horse. At ground level she had lost none of her stature, but took command of the proceedings as if born to it – which indeed she had been.

'Thank you,' she said. She surveyed the room. 'Some of you will already be aware that my father was in the Indian Civil Service in the old days, when the British ruled India. Long before any of you were born. There were only five hundred men in the ICS at that time. They ruled the entire sub-continent single handed.' From the way she spoke it was obvious that in her opinion they didn't make men like that any more.

She started the film. A small child appeared in grainy black and white. It wore a solar topee and was perched on top of an elephant.

'That's me,' she told the boys. 'Naini Tal, '29 or '30.'

A column of men marched Charlie Chaplin-like past a figure on a dais.

'That's Pops taking the salute. He always used to take the salute. People liked to have something to march past.'

A goat was led into an arena. Four Indian soldiers gathered round it. A sword flashed and the Indians leapt back to reveal the headless animal thrashing around in its own blood.

'The festival of dashera. The maharajah organised it for us. Nice little man. There'll be a cloud of dust next.' Sure enough, a white cloud filled the screen. 'You can't see much, but I can tell you under that cloud two elephants were fighting. Specially arranged for us by the rajah.'

So it went on. Lady Bullivant's mother had died young, leaving her to fill the place at her father's side as an official consort of the Indian Civil Service. From her early teens she had taken precedence over every other European memsahib in India, over most of the men as well. She had never lost the habit.

'That's my brother,' she said, of a thickset youth in straw hat and tails. 'His first day at Harrow.' She peered into the projector. 'He shouldn't have been in there at all.'

She had lived in Kenya ever since India's independence. There had once been a Sir Somebody Bullivant who had ruled natives at her side, but he had gone swiftly to his grave, leaving Lady Bullivant to enjoy an active widowhood at her farmhouse above Naivasha, surrounded by horses, dogs and flowers. She taught at Haggard Hall not for the money, but because she had nothing else to do.

Her reputation was fierce. It was said of her, and no one doubted it, that when Mau Mau terrorists had rustled cattle from her farm, she had personally tracked down the culprits at the head of a Masai war party and supervised their annihilation. She was one of those settlers who never locked a door during the Emergency, so terrified were the natives of what she might do to them.

As yet though Martin knew nothing of Lady Bullivant's former years. He saw her only as she stood before him – a beefy lady with mud-stained boots and a double chin. There was little in what he saw to suggest that she had once been a woman.

He felt a tap on his shoulder. Desmond motioned him outside.

'I want you to meet the Padre,' he said. 'Padre, this is your Mr Riddle.'

Martin remembered the pigeons. They were still in the Land-rover. He began to explain – but the Padre got in first.

'I hope you don't mind, Mr Riddle, I've just been through your luggage, looking for my squabs. I'm sorry to have to tell you that they're both dead.'

'Oh dear,' said Martin.

'Well it's a great shame, but I dare say it can't be helped.' Long years in Africa had rendered the Padre stoical. 'I understand you gave them to the servants to look after. They're wonderful people,

81

Africans, truly they are, but you can never rely on them for anything.'

Martin said nothing.

'You'll take the common entrance form tomorrow,' Desmond told him. 'Mr Waterhouse's old lot. First period's at nine o'clock. Keep them at it, don't give them a chance to brood about Smith-Baggot.'

'I won't.'

'The Padre will show you to your room. You don't play bridge, I suppose?'

'No.'

'Nobody does any more. Well I'd get an early night if I were you. You look as if you need it.'

Martin did. He could not remember when he had last been to sleep. He followed the Padre upstairs to his room, where his suit-case and Sainsbury's bag had already been laid out on the bed. It was the biggest bedroom Martin had ever been in. It boasted a zebra skin rug, a pair of stuffed oryx heads on the wall, and a brick-backed fireplace piled high with burning logs. These were tended by a grinning servant who shuffled out as the others entered.

'You get two fires a week,' the Padre told him. 'Anything more comes out of your pay. The fire in the staff room is free. I'd use that.'

A fire in Africa was a surprise. Yet it was cold enough. The sheets on the bed were turned down, and underneath them Martin counted three thick blankets.

'PT tomorrow,' the Padre went on. 'The boys do it before break-fast. You'll hear them outside your window.'

'I'm sure I shall,' said Martin.

He wished the Padre goodnight and got into bed. There was nowhere to hang his mosquito net. He lay for a while, unable to sleep, his body still spinning. Outside the window, cicadas were shrill in the darkness; on the ceiling, the oryx horns made strange shadows in the firelight. 'Twenty-four hours ago,' Martin told himself in wonder, 'I was still at Purley Way.'

Then he fell asleep.

13

High in the Aberdare mountains, Smith-Baggot too was settling down to sleep.

For an hour after sunset he had lain rigid, alert to any change in the pattern of the forest, any sudden shift that might betray a human presence other than his own. Then, working cautiously in the darkness, he had constructed a basha of magomboki shrub, a sheltered hiding place in the undergrowth indistinguishable from the surrounding foliage. He had sited it carefully, with an eye to a swift exit. It was close to a river, but not so close that the sound of water would mask any other noise, and surrounded by a thick underlay of leaves and bark so that he would leave no tracks in passing. He had also urinated methodically all round it, marking the approaches to his territory with an alien smell, a deterrent to forest creatures great and small.

It had been a long day for Smith-Baggot. It had begun shortly before dawn, when he had crept out of the dormitory and down to the headmaster's study to retrieve his .22 from the gun rack. He had unlocked the gun with no trouble and let himself out of the school building by the staff room door. From there he had made his way to the stables, where he had rolled himself in dung to confuse the pursuit. This had been his undoing, for it was at the stables that Lady Bullivant had stumbled across him. Smith-Baggot had managed to get away, but without the head start he had been counting on.

The rest of the day had shown no improvement. Every man's hand had been against him; every creature had been his enemy. Smith-Baggot was no stranger to adversity, had long become resigned to it. But to the normal instruments of oppression had been added the baying of hounds and the trill of a hunting horn,

83

twin sounds that haunted him all day, sometimes near, sometimes far, never shaken off entirely. The hounds had menaced him wherever he went, across veld and pasture, thorn and scrub, game trail and river bed. Twice he thought he had lost them, twice he had been mistaken. They had stayed with him to the end, always there, always dogging his footsteps. Not until nightfall, when he zigzagged the final few yards to the treeline of the Aberdares, had he at last reached sanctuary.

Smith-Baggot shivered. It was cold in the Aberdares and cheerless. He had not eaten all day. Tomorrow, when he ascended to the bamboo line, he would be able to light a fire, because bamboo burned without telltale smoke. For tonight though, the only refuge lay in sleep. Deep within his hide, Smith-Baggot gnawed savagely on a piece of biltong. Then he lay down and wept.

14

When he woke next morning, Martin wondered for a moment where he was. It needed the oryx heads on the wall to remind him.

He dressed quickly and found his way downstairs to the staff room. Breakfast was already laid out on the sideboard, a selection of bacon, egg and tomato in silver chafing dishes, a choice of paw paw or porridge to start with. The room was deserted except for the Padre.

'Is there any news of Smith-Baggot?' Martin asked.

'Not so far. The headmaster has gone down to Naivasha to see what he can find out. We should hear something soon. It's when we hear nothing at all that we must start to worry.'

Martin helped himself to paw paw and sat down. 'This came for you,' said the Padre.

It was a telegram. '*Good luck in your new job thinking of you always. Mum and Dad.*' The syce had collected it from the station.

'Do they run away often?' Martin asked. 'The boys, I mean?'

'Oh yes. We always have one or two every term. They don't usually get away though. Smith-Baggot is the exception rather than the rule.'

The French windows opened and Eugene Nodleman came in. He was flushed with exertion. Like all good Americans, he had jogged several miles before breakfast and composed a short paper.

'Hi,' he said to Martin. 'How you doing?'

He did not wait for a reply, but poured himself a glass of pineapple juice and swallowed a vitamin pill the size of a plover's egg.

'You're the new teacher,' he told Martin.

'Yes I am.'

'What's your field?'

'Well I don't know that I've got a field really.' Martin was disconcerted. 'I did Maths and Physics at college, if that's what you mean.'

'You read that new book by Bumschlager?'

'I don't think so.'

'*Transitions to the continuum in Time-Dependent Perturbation Theory*.'

'No, definitely not.'

'Read it,' said Eugene. 'It's good. How about Stumblebergen? *The supersymmetry of matter*.'

'I haven't read that either.'

'Basically it's the symmetry between ordinary particles of matter and exchange particles. The problem is how to identify the supersymmetric partner. It's an interesting question. But I guess you'd know all about that.'

Martin gazed wistfully at his breakfast. 'I haven't really given it much thought,' he confessed.

'Of course you have to read Stumblebergen in German to get the definitive text,' Eugene went on. 'Now in *my* work. . . .'

But he was interrupted by Lady Bullivant and her two dogs, who had followed him in through the windows. Lady Bullivant had been down to the stables and was wearing a pair of riding breeches heavily coated with blood. She was carrying a metal instrument, similar to a pair of pliers, which she banged down on the table next to Martin's side plate.

Martin did not recognise the instrument. It was an emasculator, an equine nut cracker. Lady Bullivant had been using it to geld a recalcitrant stallion.

'Sit,' she commanded the dogs. 'Sit, Nkomo. Sit, Mugabe.' Then to Martin: 'Just out from England?'

Martin nodded.

'A long time since I've been Home.' Lady Bullivant threw the dogs a kidney from the chafing dish. 'Can't say I miss it. The people are so rude. The workmen, I mean.'

'I suppose they are.'

'Mind you, they play the national anthem in England, after the film is over. They've stopped that here, you know.'

'Martin's brought some Gentleman's Relish,' the Padre told her. 'I thought we might have some later. For tea perhaps.'

'A good idea, Padre. The *pishi* can make toast.'

One of the dogs, either Mugabe or Nkomo, placed its muzzle in Martin's lap and looked speculatively at his fried egg. He surrendered a portion quietly. Really, he thought, these people weren't at all bad. They could have been much worse. He wondered if the common entrance form would be as easy to deal with.

'You'll be helping me with the first eleven for cricket,' the Padre advised him after breakfast. 'We play cricket in the English winter. It's our summer, you see.'

'I don't know very much about the game.'

'That's all right. The boys know it all. The big match is against St Brendan's. They'll tell you all about it if you let them.' The Padre was in a hurry. He was due to spend the morning at the Protestant mission. 'How are you on Guy Fawkes?'

'Guy Fawkes?'

'Bonfire night. We always have one. The headmaster has asked if you will organise it this year. The boys are making a guy and we've ordered the fireworks from Nairobi. All you have to do is see that the fire gets built.'

'I'd be delighted.'

'We usually have it down by the pavilion. Mogadishu will show you where. Is that the bell? I must go. You'll find your class past the latrines and second on the left. Keep a firm grip on them if you know what you're doing. Don't let them get away with anything.'

Martin's class inhabited a wooden hut on stilts, which had been added to the main building when it became a school. There was a blackboard at one end of the room; facing it six double desks stained with ink.

'Good morning, sir,' said twelve boys as he entered.

'Good morning,' he replied.

A pause followed as Martin took his seat at the master's table. It was bare except for a small cardboard box at the end nearest the boys. He pulled it towards him and found that it contained a board rubber and an old, dried up, dead chameleon.

'Right,' he said. 'We'd better begin. Geometry.'

'Sir.' A boy at the back had his hand up. 'Nightshade, sir. Is it true that Smith-Baggot hasn't been found yet? Is it? We heard from the syce he was still missing.'

'I don't know anything about Smith-Baggot.'

'*Please*, sir. It's important. I need to find out. He owes me two nut crunches.'

'I'm sorry, I can't help. I don't know any more than you.' Martin opened a geometry book.

'But he is missing, isn't he? Is that why the headmaster wasn't at prayers this morning?'

'Yes it is. And now can we get on with some work?'

'Sir.' This was Stephen Karanja. 'Did you know Mr Waterhouse? He was our last form master.'

'I didn't, as a matter of fact.'

'He never went to prayers either. He said they ought to be abolished.'

'He said they were the opium of the masses, sir.'

'I dare say he did,' said Martin. 'But I'm not Mr Waterhouse. I shall be doing things differently from now on.'

'Have you ever seen a tarantula?'

Martin was taken aback. 'What on earth's that got to do with anything?'

'Fife-Nugent has one in his pencil box. Go on, Fify, show us your tarantula.'

Fife-Nugent opened his box. The tarantula cowered inside. It was one of many in the school, owned and trained for the fights which took place on Saturday afternoons. The first to shed three legs was always the loser.

'I think actually you'd better put that away,' Martin told him.

'Oh go on, sir. He likes a bit of a run around.'

'Put it away.'

'I can't. He might bite me.'

'Away. And while you're at it, Fife-Nugent, you can write a hundred lines.' Martin was determined to be firm. '*No tarantulas in class*, by tonight.' He picked up the chalk. 'That goes for the rest of you too. Any more talking and you get a hundred lines.'

'Show him your praying mantis.'

'Right, Nightshade. A hundred lines. *I must not talk in class.*'

'I'm sorry.' Nightshade's tone was injured. 'I didn't realise we'd started.'

The class fell silent. Nobody moved. Martin took the dead chameleon by the tail and dropped it into the wastepaper basket. He drew a triangle on the board, looked round at the boys, and labelled it ABC.

'Now,' he told them. 'Geometry.'

The rest of the morning passed quietly enough; the threat of a hundred lines was sufficient to keep the class in check. When he emerged at the end, Martin congratulated himself on coming through his first big test with something to spare.

He went down to the pavilion as soon as lunch was over to supervise the building of the fire. The outdoor servants were already waiting for him, headed by Mogadishu. They were squatting in the dust, playing an African form of draughts under a cedar tree.

'Jambo, bwana,' said Mogadishu cheerfully.

'Jambo,' Martin replied, wary of the foreign tongue. He forced himself not to look at Mogadishu's nose. Karanja had told him that it had been eaten away by congenital syphilis.

The men had spent the morning gathering a supply of brushwood. Under Martin's direction they cleared a space in front of the pavilion and set to work to construct the bonfire. Martin led them by example, joining in the work and sharing the weight of the bulkier logs. He was assisted by Mogadishu's youngest son, a compliant two-year-old in a shirt and nothing else, staggering under a piece of leleshwa wood almost as heavy as himself. Mogadishu's youngest son possessed just the one shirt, handed down to him by two elder brothers. He changed it every birthday for a larger version.

The pyre was all but finished inside the hour. It stood ten feet

89

tall and almost as wide. It needed only a wooden stake on top to be complete.

Martin looked round for one. 'It's for the guy,' he explained.

'What is guy?' Mogadishu was curious.

'He tried to blow up Parliament. A long time ago.'

'He was English, this guy?'

'Yes he was.'

'And you are English too?'

'That's right. I came from there yesterday.'

Mogadishu followed Martin's finger northwards. 'So you are burning guy because he wanted to explode your Parliament?'

Martin nodded. 'We always do it. It's a tradition.'

Mogadishu was new to the service of the British, but eager to learn. It was his ambition that one day his two-year-old *toto* would be able to read and write and get a job in Nairobi as a clerk.

'I think perhaps guy has been in prison already,' he ventured.

'Oh he's dead. He has been, for hundreds of years.'

'I see,' said Mogadishu, not entirely truthfully. The more he studied the British, the more he realised that they were a devious people, never as straightforward as they at first appeared.

Mogadishu was still a youngish man, whose acquaintance with the British was comparatively recent. He had grown up on the Somali side of the border in that turbulent No Man's Land – ignorant of international boundaries – where Pax Britannica had never reached. He was a full-blooded Somali by birth, a Muslim warrior by inclination. He had first entered Kenya, although he did not know it, during the shifta troubles of the late 1960s. He had made an arrangement with a girl from his village and had joined a raiding party, as was customary, to bring back a pair of testicles as a gift for her father. Several times he had ventured thus across the Kenyan frontier. Several times he had returned with the members of some lonely herd boy or water gatherer pinned in triumph to his spear. He had become a man of substance in his village, buying wives and begetting children, building a hut with the dung of his own camel. He had lived well, but always restlessly, always with the urge to sharpen his spear once again, to see the light of battle one last time. This had been his undoing.

It was on a swansong raid across the frontier, a final unnecessary foray in pursuit of blood and excitement, that Mogadishu had fallen foul of Kenya's paramilitary anti-poaching unit. He had been wounded in the leg during an ambush and arrested before he could escape. He had spent the next three years in a government prison. This had been a revelation to him, for the majority of his sentence had been served in Nairobi – the first town he had ever set eyes on.

After his release he had started to walk home to Somalia, where his womenfolk had long since forgotten about him, but had got no further than the Somali village at Naivasha, a brightly coloured shanty town for migrant workers just north of the airstrip. Here he had lingered until finding a job at Haggard Hall. Here also he had found his present wife. She was a Kikuyu, a Roman Catholic, who worked in the fields behind the servants' quarters. Mogadishu had paid a heavy bride price for her, a price he was happy with at the time, but which he had subsequently come to regret. They lived now with three children in a state of pronounced marital distress.

'I think that's about it,' Martin decided. The bonfire was complete and the stake in position, ready for the guy. 'The men can knock off now.'

'But why did guy want to blow up Parliament?' Mogadishu was still curious.

'He didn't like the way the country was being run. So he tried to kill the people who were running it. He was a troublemaker, you see. A Catholic. If he'd been Church of England it would never have happened.'

This at least Mogadishu could believe. He had trouble of his own with the Catholic church. He held it to blame for the short-comings in his private life. His wife, obedient at first in all things, was no longer the woman he had married. In recent months, ever since the coming of the Irish-Italian mission to Naivasha, she had been under a spell, a trance from which Mogadishu could do nothing to rouse her. She had introduced a crucifix to their hut and a Bible; had taken to spending more and more of her time at the mission, in constant attendance on the priests. She had even allowed them to baptise Mogadishu's youngest *toto* into the Church without his knowledge and against his express command.

Mogadishu disliked the holy men. He resented the interference of strangers – infidels – in his affairs. But what rankled most about the priests, more even than the corruption of his child, was their intrusion into his priapic life. Mogadishu came of an old people, a camel-driving people: his priapic life followed traditional lines. His wife was still a pretty woman, with the Kikuyu's knack of bending down straight legged so that her buttocks rose high in the air and her dress rode up over the backs of her thighs. Observing her thus one day, Mogadishu had approached from behind and enjoyed her in the traditional Somali way. This could hardly have come as a surprise to his wife – but instead of ruminative acquiescence she had rubbed herself reproachfully and talked to him of missionaries. Certain behaviour, she had told him, was prohibited in the book of God. Certain behaviour merited a thousand Hail Marys from Father Heffernan. Mogadishu had pooh poohed this, but his wife had not been swayed. The Church's position was quite explicit. There could be no carnality of Mogadishu's sort; nor had there been, for more than a month. The situation was such, in the absence of a camel, that Mogadishu had begun to think seriously of the goat tethered in the yard.

15

Martin returned to his room for a wash. It was mid-afternoon and he was still feeling jet lagged. His work on the bonfire, at a high altitude, had proved unexpectedly demanding. He took off his shirt and soaped himself thoroughly in the basin, removing all the debris from his person. Then he lay on top of his bed and settled down to sleep.

He had not quite dropped off when the door opened and a woman came in. Martin could tell it was a woman because her high heels click-clacked noisily across the floor. He sat up at once and swung his legs off the bed.

She was in her early thirties, heavily made up, with a hairstyle that spoke of private fantasies. Martin caught a glimpse of thick ankles and a cocktail dress of some flimsy material – he guessed chiffon – that seemed wildly unsuitable for a tropical afternoon.

'Got a ciggy?' she asked. 'I hope I'm not intruding.'

Martin grabbed his shirt. 'I'm afraid I don't smoke.'

'Pity. I thought you might have some duty free. You can't get decent fags out here. I'm Mrs Fist, by the way. The matron. Pleased to meet you.'

'How do you do.' Martin was fully dressed now.

'It's Martin, isn't it? Mine's Lorraine. I'm sorry we didn't meet at breakfast. I was busy seeing to the boys.'

'That's all right.'

'I always see to the boys at breakfast. Morning surgery. Coughs, colds, ear ache. That sort of thing.'

'So I come to you if I feel ill?'

'Not really. I don't know much about it. I was on the airlines before I came here. A hostess. Only it got too much. I could still be one, you know, honestly I could. But I was on the long haul routes and it played hell with my cycle. It just wasn't worth it in the end.' Mrs Fist eased her dress into Martin's armchair. 'So I came here. Without my husband, of course. There's just me and my little boy now. He's almost eighteen months.'

'And do you like it here?'

'It's all right. It's a bit different from what I'm used to. Servants and all. We were from Croydon originally. But the Africans are very friendly – they'll do anything to please and they always say Jambo.'

'Yes I've noticed,' agreed Martin. 'They do seem very cheerful. What about the whites, though? Major Gale. What's he like?'

'He treats me like dirt, always has. But I like him. He's a man, if you know what I mean.'

'And Lady Bullivant?'

'That woman! Don't talk to me about her!' Mrs Fist sniffed. 'Who she thinks she is I don't know. Stuck up old cow. Carries on as if she owns the place.'

'She does seem to have been around a long time.'

'The British should stick together out here, that's what I say. We're all in the same boat. If it wasn't for us the Africans would be speaking some language they didn't understand.

'And those awful dogs of hers. They get over everything. She took them into the dormitory once – teaching them to retrieve. She hid a dead bird under one of the beds and turned the dogs loose. Blood and feathers everywhere. You never saw such a mess.'

Mrs Fist inspected her ankles. Martin related the story of his own first encounter with Lady Bullivant. He spoke of the hunting horn and Smith-Baggot. Mrs Fist nodded in sympathy.

'That's her. She's a bit cracked, if you ask me. I blame the altitude.'

'Does anybody know what's happened to Smith-Baggot, as a matter of interest?'

'No. The police say if they haven't found him by tomorrow he'll have to be presumed dead. Poor little sod. They were all against him, you know.'

'They must have been.'

'Are you going to the party on bonfire night?'

'Yes,' said Martin modestly. 'I'm organising it.'

'They're having a minute's silence for him if he hasn't turned up. The headmaster is arranging it. Sort of a memorial service before the fireworks begin.' Mrs Fist uncurled herself. 'Well I can't sit around here all day. I must be going.' She tapped Martin's sleeve. 'Nice to meet you. I'll see you again. I hope you last longer than Waterhouse did. He was an odd fellow. He never really fitted in here.'

'I'm not sure that I will either.'

'Nobody does,' said Mrs Fist. 'That's half the trouble.'

16

Bonfire night carried the possibility of a light drizzle, for the November rains were under way and there was a touch of dampness in the air. Several times during the afternoon Martin looked up from his preparations to assess the porpoise-coloured clouds above the Aberdares. Once or twice he thought he heard thunder. But the clouds remained distant and the rain gods held their peace. By nightfall, when the school trooped across the playing fields to assemble by the pavilion, the weather was still intact.

Desmond opened the proceedings by the light of a hurricane lamp.

'Before we begin,' he told the boys, 'I think we might spare a few thoughts for Smith-Baggot. Whatever has happened to him, and we still don't know exactly what, the time does seem to have come when we must face up to facts and assume the worst.'

The row of faces behind the Catherine wheels adopted a solemn, Sunday morning expression.

'He was a foolish boy in many ways, but a likeable one. I know I speak for everyone here when I say we were all fond of him. He was a valued member of our little community. Not academically gifted perhaps, but a mainstay of the sharpshooting team and a person who could always be relied upon to try his utmost. A lone wolf who would always pitch in when needed. There are certain qualities we try to inculcate here, such as courage and self-reliance, which Smith-Baggot possessed in abundance. We shall miss him.' Desmond studied his flock. 'So I think it would be appropriate if we now bowed our heads in silence for a moment and remembered Smith-Baggot as we all knew him – as pupil, as team mate, and ultimately I feel sure, as a good friend.'

Everyone clasped their hands in front of them and looked at the ground. The hurricane lamp was besieged by insects. Martin stood with Eugene and the Padre, Mrs Fist with her infant son in her arms. The African servants formed a separate group the other side of the pavilion, not quite sure what the silence was about, but determined not to miss the show. Mogadishu had brought his *toto*, who clung to his father's knees and fidgeted spasmodically.

'And now,' continued Desmond after a decent interval, 'perhaps we can begin the fireworks. Mr Riddle, would you do the honours?'

Martin stepped forward. He had worked hard that afternoon, nailing Catherine wheels to planks of wood, arranging rockets in bottles, assembling piles of sparklers for distribution to the boys. Conscious of a critical audience, he produced a taper and began to set light to his handiwork.

Soon the air was filled with exploding rockets. Martin had planned the sequence carefully. An initial burst in the sky, then a few Roman candles and jumping jacks, then another aerial display leading up to a finale of sorts and the igniting of the bonfire. He had written down the running order on a piece of graph paper which he kept with him as he hurried between the bottles.

'A good display, Riddle,' Desmond congratulated him halfway through. 'What was that last one that went up?'

Martin consulted his list. 'It was either a Coloured Niagara or a Jewelled Pyramid,' he reported.

'Good, good. Keep it up.'

After the fireworks, the sparklers. Every boy was entitled to five each. A handful were also distributed to the African children, some twenty or thirty piccaninnies who came forward shyly to receive the gift. Mogadishu's *toto* took his gingerly, unsure how to react. He waved it experimentally in a half circle, then broke into a broad smile.

Martin lit the fire. The guy was already in place on top, an awkward creation with a grinning rugby ball for a head. It was dressed in a pullover and a floppy hat of Mrs Fist's. Also a pair of Smith-Baggot's khaki trousers that he wouldn't be needing any more.

The fire burned swiftly, for despite the promise of rain the wood was dry and free of sap. The flames lit up the faces of the boys, intent on the destruction of the guy. A cheer went up when it caught light. Another when it toppled forward and was lost to view among the flickering branches.

'This guy,' Mogadishu asked Martin. 'You burn him because he was a Catholic?'

'More or less. His religion was at the root of the trouble.'

'They burn Catholics often in England?'

'This one they did. Hanged, drew and quartered him as well.'

'What is quartered?'

'It's kind of a folk custom,' explained Eugene. 'Part of the British national psyche. Socially and culturally, November the Fifth goes way back. Guy Fawkes is just the focus for a ritual fire worship that can be traced all the way to the Druids, if not beyond. It's a tribal thing.'

'Rather like Burns night,' suggested the Padre.

'Oh I don't think the two can be compared. Burns after all is a national hero. The aetiology is quite different.'

The fire was dying now, accompanied by the pungent smell of burnt fireworks. A light rain had begun to fall, confirming the prognosis of the afternoon. It was time for the boys to be in bed. Eugene, who was master on duty, called the roll and shepherded them back to the dormitories in the main building.

'Why does he have *Tufts* written across his chest?' Martin asked the Padre.

'He says it's a university.'

From the servants' quarters, a furlong away behind the pavilion, came the sudden barking of a pack of dogs. It was accompanied by a woman's voice raised in alarm.

'Something happening,' said Desmond. 'Mogadishu, go and see.'

Mogadishu was away five minutes. When he returned, it was to fetch Desmond. '*Kuja, bwana. Shauri ya chui.*'

'A leopard,' said Desmond. 'God, what a bore.'

Holding up the hurricane lamp, he hurried after Mogadishu. Nothing happened for a quarter of an hour, during which Martin wondered how a leopard could possibly be a bore. Then Desmond came back.

'It's a leopard, all right. Taken one of the pi-dogs. You could see the pugs clear as day.'

'Just down there?' Martin asked in disbelief.

'Yes. Happens quite often. The more the merrier, frankly. I can't bear pi-dogs.'

'All the same, headmaster, it could be a nuisance.' The Padre sounded a warning note. 'We don't want another incident, so soon after Smith-Baggot.'

'There's nothing that can be done tonight. The leopard won't kill again for a while. I'll get down there in the morning and see if I can follow it up.'

Martin accompanied the others back to the staff room. He strained his ears for the leopard, but heard only the ubiquitous cicadas in the undergrowth. He found it hard to take a leopard in his stride. The casual way everyone else treated big game, as simply an adjunct to everyday life, filled him with curiosity. Big game was surely a miracle, something to be marvelled at. He could not understand how his companions could remain so unmoved.

When he got back to his room, he locked the door in case Mrs Fist should feel like a smoke and sat down to write to his parents. He had not written since his postcard from Nairobi. He told them everything that had happened to him at Haggard Hall. Smith-Baggot, the rhino droppings, how he had carried a rifle and led a wild tribesman through the jungle. He mentioned the leopard in passing and hinted that he might have to do something about it in the morning. '*The headmaster says that if we find the pi-dog we can dose it with strychnine,*' he wrote. '*Leopards always return to their kill, and that's the way to get them. It happens a lot out here.*'

Out here. He wondered how his letter would go down in Purley Way. Probably his mother would read it to Gran and then to Mrs Simmonds at number fourteen. Martin sealed the envelope and switched off the light. Somehow Purley Way and all its works suddenly seemed very far away.

99

17

In the darkness the rain gave play to its true feelings. It plunged down with all the drama of the tropics, harsh and unforgiving, furious and implacable, as if a war had suddenly been declared. Over the mountains it turned rapidly to hail. In the mossy glades of the Aberdares, unprotected by forest, it flattened the undergrowth in swathes and drove the animals to panic, crushing the life out of the smaller ones which failed to find shelter in time.

Smith-Baggot had found shelter of a sort in the bamboo belt, ten thousand feet up and cold enough for a frost in the early morning. He had been prepared for the cold, but not for the hail. He had built himself a raised platform of bamboo, a feathery nest to protect him from the worst of the elements; next to it a fire on which he had warmed the last of his biltong. Tomorrow he would have to fish for trout or expend one of his precious bullets on a duiker or bushbuck – if he could find one at this height. The hour after dawn was the best time, before the game went to ground.

Smith-Baggot turned up the collar of his shirt and waited for the hail to stop. Everything he possessed was wet except for his rifle, which was wrapped in a waterproof binding. He always carried it muzzle down to keep rust out of the barrel. He was tired, for he had been climbing steadily all day. He had a headache from the altitude and a raging stomach from a diet of raw meat. Tomorrow he would reach the saddle of the mountains, the bleak moorlands – virtually devoid of vegetation – that led over the top and down again to the plains of Naro Moru. He would be home in a couple of days, three at most. For the moment he was still on the dark side of the Aberdares, the side that looked towards Naivasha and Haggard Hall. Smith-Baggot had observed Martin's bonfire from afar, a tiny point of flame in a mass of darkness. He had not known what it meant though, because he had no idea of the date.

His bowels woke him twice during the remainder of the night; again at dawn. He rose stiff and sore, ready for the upward climb. A heavy mist overnight had reduced visibility to fifty yards – the ground was rimmed with frost. Once or twice during the dark hours he had heard a rumbling sound nearby, which he had correctly identified as an elephant's stomach. Now he saw them through the mist, a herd of four or five, descending towards the lusher grazing which rain had brought to the lower slopes. All around them the air crackled with pistol shots as the gas-filled bamboo exploded in the warmth of the new day.

Smith-Baggot trudged on. He reached the moorlands, an Alpine world of groundsel and lobelia, far removed from the BBC Africa of the plains. Ahead lay the twin glaciers of Mount Kenya, home of the god Ngai, a sight familiar to him from the windows of his room at home. He was over the worst of the mountains. On a spur below he could see the national park track and a game warden's Landrover emerging minutely from the Treetops salient. He knew where he was now. Twenty miles to go, all of it downhill.

For the first time since his escape, he wondered what sort of welcome he would receive at Naro Moru. His father would not be pleased to see him; nor would his mother. They had pinned all their hopes on Eton. It was the family place. But Smith-Baggot did not care. Nothing bothered him any more. Nothing could touch him. It was enough just to be going home.

18

The day after Guy Fawkes, Desmond rose earlier than usual and was already out of his bath when the houseboy called with tea at seven a.m. He was filling the pockets of his shooting coat with ammunition and a small bottle of strychnine to dose the remains of the pi-dog. Last night's leopard would be long gone, its tracks obliterated by the rain, but it was always conceivable that the dog had been lodged in some convenient tree, to be retrieved later.

The Ndorobo tracker was waiting outside the staff room door. Together they walked down to the servants' quarters, a rank collection of huts backing on to a wide copse of trees, obvious country for a leopard. The pi-dog must have been an easy prey; it had belonged to a pack of thirty or forty, verminous creatures, brimming with ticks and lice. Desmond had made it a rule that any dog straying from the servants' quarters would be shot on sight. More than once he had also drowned them in the lake.

The tracker had already cast around for the leopard without success. The pugs last night had led westward, away from the trees, but leopards were notorious for doubling back where they were least expected. For form's sake Desmond and the tracker made a show of following it up, pursuing a non-existent spoor to demontrate that something was being done. They set off at a cautious pace, studying the fork of every tree they came to for a half-eaten carcass, or even a sleeping leopard. They found nothing. Out of sight of the huts, they abandoned the search and lit up cigarettes.

'He'll be away now,' said Desmond. 'Out in the *bundu* somewhere.'

'*Ndio*,' the tracker agreed. '*Na kwisha kwenda.*'

'Think we'll see him again?'

'Eeeeh,' said the tracker, which could have been yes or no.

Desmond examined the sky. 'It's going to rain again. We should get back.' He shouldered his rifle. 'We'll drop in on Mzee first. He might know something. If there's been a leopard, he'll have heard about it.'

Mzee lived on a patch of high ground above a farm track. He was an ancient Masai, reputedly a hundred years old but probably no more than eighty. He was an old timer of repellent appearance, a male Gagool with niveous hair, a shrunken chest and two yellow teeth in an otherwise empty head. He was blind in one eye, half-blind in the other. His ear lobes hung down to his shoulders and were pierced with circular discs of tin. He wore a woolly hat, a red blanket and a pair of sandals made from an old car tyre.

They found him outside his hut, squatting on his hunkers in the dirt. He had squatted thus for most of the century, missing little that went on around the shores of the lake. It had been Uganda when he had first squatted there, but later the border had been shifted to the north. He was so old that he could remember the outbreak of war with the wa-Germani, when all the English had ridden through the night to attack their fellow bwanas and seize their cattle. The first war, that is. His memory had clouded thereafter.

He was not alone when they arrived. He was with Eugene, who was sitting cross-legged beside him.

'Hi,' said Eugene. 'Mzee and I are just getting started.'

A tape recorder whirred between them. Eugene was recording the old man's memoirs for his thesis. Mzee was part of the old Africa, a window on a world that had all but vanished. He was invaluable to Eugene. His powers of recall stretched back as far as the Masai *laibon* Lenana, a famous chief who had died in 1911. Mzee had known him personally.

'And that's not all,' Eugene enthused. 'He remembers Karen Blixen too, clear as a bell. He's a gold mine, this guy, I'm telling you.'

'Don't tip him too much.' Desmond had once asked Mzee if he remembered Lord Nelson and Sir Walter Raleigh. He remembered them well.

On leopards he was less forthcoming. There had been none, so far as he knew. If one turned up though, he promised the bwana would be the first to hear about it.

'He'll let you know,' said Eugene. 'He's a good old boy.'

'I hope so.'

'He's going to fix me up with a sacrifice. A goat. I'm going to get the whole ceremony on film. Maybe even the National Geographic.'

19

It rained for the rest of that morning and for enough of the afternoon to cancel the day's cricket. This was a blow to the first eleven, for the St Brendan's match was drawing near, the most important fixture of the season. St Brendan's was always the team to beat, a formidable enemy of long standing – 'Harrow to our Eton', as Desmond explained it to Martin. The first eleven needed all the practice they could get. From the shelter of the pavilion, they cast accusing glances at the sky and fretted.

Once it was clear that no play would be possible, the Padre gave them a pep talk instead.

'I don't have to remind you what happened last year,' he reminded them. 'We were beaten fair and square, on our own ground too. Thirteen all out, if I remember rightly.'

'It was their bowler, sir,' said Nightshade. 'He took six for seven.'

'Well he isn't there any more, I happen to know. He's gone on to Sherborne. So there's no excuse for anything like that happening again.'

Karanja, who was scorer, turned up the offending game in his book. 'There were two run-outs in our innings and four ducks,' he reported. 'Three of them lbw.'

'Batting,' agreed the Padre, 'that's our weakness.'

'And catching, sir.'

'And catching. Catches win matches. Ask Mr Riddle. He'll show you as soon as the rain stops.'

But the rain did not stop. Instead the Padre dismissed the team and seized Martin by the arm. 'Come and see my birds,' he told him.

St Brendan's lay a hundred miles up-country, even further from a telephone than Haggard Hall. The only practical way of following the game's progress, for those not travelling with the team, was by carrier pigeon. The Padre was planning to take a dozen with him, to be released in pairs at hourly intervals. This was a sensible number, for about one in every two would be killed on the way back, by hawks or other birds of prey. The quest for up-to-the-minute sporting information demanded a kill ratio of fifty per cent, a statistic not always appreciated – in the Padre's opinion – by those who benefited from it.

Covering their heads with cricket pads, he and Martin hurried through the downpour to the pigeon loft. They found Mogadishu sheltering underneath. He too was waiting for the rain to stop so that he could go out and water the garden.

'Good man,' the Padre told him.

In the loft, they were deluged by birds.

'Know anything about pigeon racing?' the Padre asked.

'Not a thing,' said Martin.

'Speed is the essence. One wants the birds home as soon as possible. I've always found that the Belgian method gets the best results.'

'The Belgian method?'

'You mate a young cock bird, first time he's ever been in love, then tear the two of them apart just before the race. The last he knows, another cock is moving in on the object of his affections. He'll perform miracles to get home again quickly. It never fails. You'll see.'

The Padre sought an example and found it in Siege of Paris, a virgin Antwerp of considerable promise. The Padre had high hopes of him for St Brendan's.

'I'll show you what I mean,' he said. 'Come on, Paris, it's your birthday. I know just the right hen for you.'

With panderous hands he produced a soft plump Dewlap in the pink of condition and introduced her to the young male. Siege of Paris blinked. His head came up; he studied this phenomenon with

106

consummate interest. The Padre stepped back, reluctant to intrude further, leaving it to the Dewlap to make the running. She was skilled in the arts of courtship. With her encouragement the air quickly filled with the beat of lovers' wings and the frenzied, inimitable sound of 'treading' – music to the Padre's ears. Music also to Siege of Paris. The Padre waited for him to gain in confidence. Then, as nirvana approached, he got down the walking stick he used for the purpose and inserted it deftly between the two birds.

'See what I mean?' he told Martin. 'I think we'll stop it just there.'

20

Siege of Paris was understandably bitter at this; but there was little he could do. They left him to his own reflections and climbed down. Mogadishu was still underneath, still sheltering from the rain.

'Any news of the leopard?' Martin asked.

'*Hapana*.' Mogadishu shook his head.

'All well though?' said the Padre. 'No real damage down at the huts?'

Mogadishu shrugged. Actually all was far from well in his own household. He had had trouble with his wife again last night, the same trouble as before. He had chased her round the fire with his herd stick to bring her to her senses, but she had clutched her rosary to her breast and defied him to do his worst. The magic beads had put the fear of God into Mogadishu. He had stormed out in a state of high excitement and given the goat a surprise it would never forget. But this was none of the Padre's business.

'Almost time for tea.' The Padre peered up at the clouds. 'When *will* it stop raining?'

He and Martin dashed off in the direction of the staff room. Mogadishu watched them go, though without seeing anything. He was chewing over the events of Guy Fawkes night, thinking about the Catholic missionaries. He was wondering if they had put a curse on his wife, a *thahu* to make her cold in bed. Among the Christian Kikuyu, anything seemed possible.

What kind of people were they, these priests who made trouble between a man and his wife? What kind of people who sought to dictate the hows and whys of something so fundamentally private? Mogadishu spat sourly. It was a rum world that allowed the

Catholic fathers to take his woman away from him, and her all bought and paid for. A rum world indeed.

He was still brooding along these lines when the sun came out at last, followed by the twitter of birdsong. It was definitely time for tea now. Lady Bullivant appeared around the corner of the stables, followed by her dogs, en route for the staff room. She carried a pair of secateurs in one hand, a basket of flowers in the other. Years ago she had attended a garden party at Buckingham Palace, returning with a geranium cutting whose progeny had taken root all over Kenya. The bed outside the staff room was full of them. It was part of Mogadishu's job to see that they were watered properly, a task he now hastily undertook.

'Talk to them, Mogadishu,' Lady Bullivant told him. 'Always talk to the flowers. That's how to make them grow.'

'*Ndio memsabu.*' Mogadishu swallowed his *khat* and addressed a few words to the geraniums in Somali. They showed no perceptible increase in stature.

Lady Bullivant swept on. Once she was out of sight, Mogadishu dropped the hose and returned to his own thoughts. He should never have married outside his own people; he could see that now. Kikuyu women were different to Somalis, more independent, more inclined to argue over the cooking pots. Mogadishu would never have tolerated such recalcitrance in a woman of his own kind. There was the goat too. It was written in the Scriptures that a goat (or camel) which has been defiled must be moved to another village or otherwise disposed of. The procedure was laid down in Islamic law. Whether he wanted to or no, Mogadishu had little choice but to get rid of his most valuable animal. *Allah!* What a lot of trouble the priests had caused!

21

The Padre had gone to his room to change into dry clothes, so Martin was alone in the staff room when Lady Bullivant entered.

'Settling in?' she asked.

'More or less.'

'It's a good thing you're interested in pigeons. The Padre needs someone to share his enthusiasm with.'

Lady Bullivant rang the bell for tea. After an interval, a houseboy appeared.

'Yes. *Leti chai, mara moja*. And something for the dogs.'

'I'm sorry, *memsabu*, there is no tea. Memsahib Fist is not here yet.'

'What's Mrs Fist got to do with it?'

'She has the keys, *memsabu*. To the go-down.'

A search revealed Mrs Fist in Matron's room, supervising a nappy change on her son.

'What's this about no tea?'

'I'm keeping hold of the keys. I don't trust them in the kitchen.'

'Nonsense. Give them to me. I shall see to it.'

'I'm sorry.' Mrs Fist maintained her grip. 'I'll be there in a minute. I won't be long.'

Master Fist's nappy was being changed by a black *ayah*. Lady Bullivant had never had a baby herself, but this did not prevent her from being an authority on child care.

'You shouldn't change it like that,' she told the woman. 'You're doing it all wrong. Here, I'll show you.'

She slipped the nappy between the child's legs. His penis, hitherto dormant, reared up into an erection all of an inch long. Lady Bullivant looked at Mrs Fist.

'Come outside,' she said.

They went into the corridor. 'Don't ever let the *ayah* see him like that again. It gives them the wrong idea. Makes them think Europeans are the same as they are.'

'She's a good *ayah*. I've got no complaints.'

'You mustn't allow her to get above herself. It does no good in the long run.'

'She takes good care of Darren.'

'I dare say. But she mustn't get ideas. When you've been out here as long as I have. . . .'

22

Mrs Fist retreated to the kitchen. Tea was served. There was toast, Gentleman's Relish, a pot of guava jam; two green lemons for slicing.

'I'll pour,' said Lady Bullivant.

Desmond came late. He had had a busy afternoon in his study, catching up on his correspondence. Karanja's father had sent him another letter about ragging.

'I suppose we'd better answer it this time, Padre. I wonder if you'd drop him a line?'

'What shall I say?'

'Oh I don't know. Ragging's nothing to worry about. Tell him his son's developed an interest in the Romantic poets and we're all very pleased.'

Eugene was late too. He had spent all day with Mzee. It had taken a long time because the Masai like to talk about everything under the sun before coming to the point, a process that can last an hour or so or a couple of days. Bit by bit however the information had begun to flow and a picture had emerged of life as Mzee had known it, a cultural experience rich in ethnicity.

'You know what the Masai call white men?' he told the others. '*Ilorida n'jekat*. The people who block up their farts.' He dipped his knife into the relish. 'Because they wear clothes, you see.'

'A forthright people.' The Padre decided not to finish his tea. 'We tried to recruit them into the KAR once, but we could never persuade them to wear trousers.'

'They never wear anything much,' said Desmond. 'Ignorant bastards.'

'Fine warriors,' Eugene protested. 'Like the Apache used to be.' He was pleased with his day's work. He saw Mzee as the raw

112

material for a dissertation, a primary source all to himself. Mzee would be dead soon; then he would have no existence other than c.f. Nodleman E. *They spat in my face: My brothers the Masai* (the current title of his book). It was immortality of a sort.

'What's the story on your goat sacrifice?' Desmond asked.

'It's all arranged. Soon as I produce the goat, Mzee takes me into the bush and we break its bones, one by one. The whole ritual, specially for me.'

'*You* produce the goat?'

'Mogadishu does. He just sold me one. That's why I'm late.'

'It's not like Mogadishu to part with a goat.'

'I sweet talked him into it. He didn't want to sell at first, but I won him round. You have to know how to handle these people.'

Eugene gathered up his tapes after tea and went over to his tent to spend the rest of the evening working on his dissertation. It lay in box files under his bed, heavily cross referenced, a monument to his time in Africa.

Eugene's was a big tent, large enough to accommodate a desk, filing cabinet and canvas stool, along with his back pack and safari gear. At present it was awash with mud, a legacy of the weather. During the last drought it had been invaded by locusts, a windfall which Desmond had turned to Biblical account by serving them to the school for supper. They tasted of roast chestnuts. Eugene had joined in the feast: he was interested in culinary experience. Behind his desk he kept a gourd of cow's milk, blood, wood ash and urine, a Masai staple which he had not yet nerved himself to try.

He squelched across the mud and sat down at his typewriter. He was planning to begin Chapter Three tonight. '*The lost legion of Mark Anthony?*'

'*The Masai are a Hamitic people from the waters of the upper Nile,*' he wrote. '*Their precise origins are lost in the mists of time, but in bone structure and physiognomic detail Bilderbeyer has shown that they strongly resemble the indigenous peoples of southern Europe. Except for their pigmentation, they might easily pass as modern day Italians. Could they be the descendants of*

Mark Anthony's personal troops, forced to remain in hiding after the battle of Actium 31 BC?

'There is a wealth of evidence to effectively legitimize this hypothesis. The spear, belt, scabbard, sandals and short stabbing sword of the Masai are common also to the Roman legionary. The overlapping shields of the Masai battle formation are obviously inherited from the testudo, c.f. Bilderbeyer, passim. But the crucial evidence comes from my own researches, which have revealed a strong oral tradition in favor of an ancient laibon named Maa Kuss N'Tonus, famed for his skill in battle. . . .'

And so on, deep into the night. Eugene's fingers twinkled across the keys; the pages fell like ticker tape. Beneath his feet, Mogadishu's goat dozed contentedly, unaware of the dreadful fate that lay in store for it. When it grew dark, he pumped up the hurricane lamp and closed the flap of his tent to keep out the mosquitoes. Now and then he opened it again to snuff the evening air, the inimitable air of Africa, leavened by the distant whoop whoop of some jungle creature and the measured tones of the BBC World Service emanating faintly from the veranda of Desmond's private rooms. It was a fine night, a night for the National Geographic Magazine. 'From my camp on the Masai steppe,' Eugene thought idly, 'I could hear the roar of lions and the terrified bark of zebras desperate to escape their destiny. Leopards growled, hyenas chuckled; the night pulsated with the sound of a thousand deaths.'

He looked at the sky. The rain clouds had parted and the Southern Cross was just visible. There was no moon.

He looked at the darkness across the steppe. A light was blossoming some miles away, a barely discernible flicker of turbulence in the void.

'That the Masai should have come from Egypt is not as far fetched as it sounds. We know from Ptolemy that ancient travelers had penetrated as far as Uganda's legendary Mountains of the Moon. . . .'

The flame was larger now, a fire of some kind. So far as Eugene could judge, it was in the open country beyond Naivasha, a hut perhaps or a native shamba. He could not tell which.

Martin had seen it too. He put his head in to seek Eugene's

advice. 'Oughtn't we to do something?'

'I guess,' said Eugene. His mind was still on Chapter Three.

'Perhaps we should go and tell the headmaster.'

They went across to Desmond and found him nursing a tumbler of gin. 'A little late for November the Fifth,' he said.

'Maybe it's a bush fire?'

'Wrong time of year. You don't get them in the rains.'

A sofa creaked. Martin recognised Mrs Fist in the shadows.

'Or a cleansing ceremony?' Eugene suggested. 'Evil spirits. Burning the hut to get rid of the *thahu*.'

'Possibly.' Desmond fetched his binoculars. 'It's definitely a building of some kind. You can see the roof.'

'What kind of building? What's out there anyhow?'

'Kukes, I should think. That's Kikuyu land.'

'They'll be okay then.' Eugene was still thinking about Ptolemy.

'Odd though. A hut burning in this weather.'

The flames grew. Desmond put down his binoculars and lit a cheroot. He was thoughtful. Mrs Fist tucked up her legs invitingly and made room for him on the sofa. Desmond poured them both another drink and sat down with one hand on her knee.

'Very odd,' he said.

Presently he switched off the BBC.

'Unlike their Bantu neighbors, the Masai are a thin-lipped people, further evidence that. . . .'

23

It was a week before they learned that the Catholic mission had burned to the ground. The Padre brought the news. He had heard it from Father Heffernan, whom he had met by chance in Naivasha.

'It started in the chapel apparently. Went up straight away. There was nothing anyone could do.'

'Ashes to ashes,' said Desmond. 'Why the chapel in particular?'

'A burning candle. At least that's what they think.'

'Anybody hurt?'

'There was no one there at the time. The place was deserted. That's what's so peculiar about the candle.'

'A bad *shauri*.' Desmond was intrigued. 'What about those priests? What do they make of it?'

'Father Heffernan says they've lost everything. Their vestments, their Bibles, their piece of the True Cross. The holy water they brought back from the Jordan. All their communion wafers. Everything they've worked for has gone for nothing.'

'Padre, I do believe you're enjoying this!'

'Well you know, headmaster, I can't help feeling that it's a judgment on Father Heffernan in a way. His approach has always been a little . . . *doctrinaire* for the Africans. If I've learned one thing since I've been out here it's that you can't rush people. You must let them come to Christianity at their own pace. I've sometimes felt with the Catholic church that they're simply asking the natives to exchange one lot of superstitions for another.'

'I know what you mean. They're a rum lot. I knew a man from Ampleforth once. . . .'

And the leopard killed again. Another pi-dog. It came soon after

116

dark, while the cooking fires were still burning, and snatched a pregnant bitch from behind one of the huts. It was gone again in seconds.

'There was nothing I could do,' Desmond said afterwards. 'By the time I got there it was all over. You wouldn't have known it, though. Dogs barking, children screaming. The place was in an uproar.'

Lady Bullivant was unsympathetic. 'They love a good drama, the servants. A lot of fuss over nothing, if you want my opinion.'

24

Poor Father Heffernan! *Pro Ecclesia et Pontifice*! The Padre could scarcely contain his glee. The prayers he offered for his Catholic colleagues that evening were lavish in their condolence, but he could not rid himself of the suspicion that the Almighty (and Omniscient) would not take his commiserations altogether in the spirit in which they had been intended. So he salved his conscience by sending Father Heffernan a generous cheque for the rebuilding fund. In the circumstances, as he wrote in his covering note, it was the least he could do.

He was still in jaunty mood next morning when he roused the first eleven for the journey to St Brendan's.

'On the road by seven-thirty,' he told them. 'You've all got clean kit? Plenty of Meltonian, flannels properly dhobied? Open your bowels then and get on the bus. Today we smite the Philistines. I can feel it in my bones.'

The Padre's pigeons had already been packed for the journey. They were peering through the grille of their travelling cage, all twelve of them, gloomily confident that something awful was about to happen. The Padre had seen to it that the view from their cage was a restricting one. All they had to look at was Siege of Paris's hen, occupying a nesting box in full view of her erstwhile mate: in full view also of another cock bird which the Padre now slyly introduced into the proceedings.

This second cock was a fine specimen, a confident, swaggering brute with a big ruff – just the sort to set Siege of Paris's teeth on edge. The Padre tipped him into the hen's box. He swelled up at once and began to strut to and fro, pacing for all he was worth, giving her the full masculine treatment. The hen bird preened happily. Siege of Paris goggled through the bars and fought to escape. The perfidy of womankind was new to him – he could scarcely believe his eyes.

'That should do it,' the Padre thought. He allowed Siege of Paris one last, despairing glance and picked up the cage. The hen continued to flaunt herself. Siege of Paris struggled against the bars, imploring her to reconsider. His fellow inmates gave him their sympathy. A rumble of disapproval arose and showed no sign of abating as the Padre loaded them into the minibus.

'Check the loft every hour,' he told Martin, who had come to see them off. 'I'll let the first birds out at eleven, when we know who's won the toss. They'll do forty m.p.h., more if there's a tailwind. You should start hearing from them at lunch.'

'Right.'

'And make sure they have something to eat when they get in. They'll be exhausted. Takes a lot out of them, this heat.'

The boys squeezed into the bus. Fife-Nugent and Nightshade sat in front, next to the Padre; the rest of the team in the back. Karanja, as scorer, was relegated to the rear window. He found a niche on top of the pigeons and made V signs through the glass at those who were staying behind.

'Play up,' Desmond told them from the front door. 'England expects, and all that.'

'Play up,' shouted a crowd of pyjama-clad figures from the dormitory.

'I hope they win,' said Martin, who had caught something of the prevailing enthusiasm.

'A dreadful game.' Desmond waved magisterially at the departing bus. 'I was always a wet bob myself. I never could understand why anybody entirely sober should want to play cricket.'

It was Martin's turn to see up the boys' breakfast. In the Padre's absence he sat at the senior table, among the prefects, distributing porridge from an enormous vat brought in by two of the servants. The table was monastic in design and gleamed with athletic silverware – the Armstrong Memorial Cup, the Bullivant Cup for riding, various trophies for football and cricket. Above it the high vaulted ceiling stretched away to an infinity occupied only by a chameleon catching flies with its tongue and a family of bats which roosted undisturbed among the rafters. The dining hall had once been Lord Dunsinane's pièce de resistance – his coat of arms was carved in stone above the fireplace – and had lost little of its lustre over the years.

It was a sausage day as well as porridge. For a while conversation among the boys was limited to monosyllables and a squabble over who would have Nightshade's in his absence. With the marmalade, however, they began to talk more freely.

'What do you think our chances are, sir? Of beating St Brendan's.'

'I really don't know. It all depends, doesn't it?'

'The Padre says we'll beat them hollow if we play an attacking game. We've got to go out and look for the ball. That's what he says.'

It was the same during morning school. Martin taught geometry to the common entrance form, maths and algebra to the lower boys. He stood in for the Padre's English class and read from the poems of Sir Henry Newbolt. But nobody paid any attention. All eyes were on the pigeon loft.

'What time is it, sir?'

'Eleven-fifteen.'

'They'll have started now, won't they?'

Twice Martin went to the loft to look for news. Twice he returned empty handed. Around lunchtime he was joined by a small but determined band of enthusiasts who established themselves on the high ground with binoculars and an old naval telescope borrowed from somebody's father. A compass revealed the direction of St Brendan's. The enthusiasts settled down to wait.

Before long they were rewarded with the sight of a tiny feathered object streaking across the lake, the light glinting on its wings as it sped south. It flew low and fast, like a fighter plane, making straight for the loft. A cheer went up as it touched down, moderated only slightly when it was realised that the bird had settled on the roof, out of everyone's reach.

'Come on, bird,' coaxed Martin. 'Come on down.'

The pigeon looked at him, shifted position and vented its feelings in the usual manner.

'Come *on*, for goodness' sake!'

The bell went for lunch. Martin rattled the corn bucket. The pigeon appeared not to hear, but remained aloof on its perch, deaf to all entreaty. It stayed there another five minutes before dropping down in its own time and slipping in to the loft.

Martin followed it inside and emerged in triumph with a tiny slip of paper.

'What does it say, sir?'

'It says.' He cleared his throat. '*Hope this reaches you. Lot of hawks about. We lost the toss and they have put us in.*'

'*We lost the toss!*' The word was out. It spread rapidly, on running feet, from one end of the school to the other.

Martin pinned the message to the notice board. 'We lost the toss,' he told Desmond in passing. 'St Brendan's have put us in.'

He went to wash his hands. On the way back he bumped into Eugene.

'We lost the toss,' said Eugene.

'I know. I got the message.'

'But what does it mean?'

'It means we have to bat when we wanted to field.'

They went in to lunch. The boys' conversation, as at breakfast, was exclusively confined to cricket. Not even the marauding leopard or Smith-Baggot's escape received anything more than a cursory mention.

Afterwards Martin went again to the loft. The band of enthusiasts had swelled considerably. Half the school was watching as he put his hand into the box, like a bingo caller, and withdrew the message.

'We're 53 all out,' he announced. 'Nightshade 22.'

Applause greeted this statement. Fifty-three was a respectable total, enough to give the team a commanding lead.

'What about Fife-Nugent, sir?' someone asked. 'What did he score?'

'I don't know. The Padre doesn't say.'

The afternoon wore on. The enthusiasts maintained their vigil, quartering the sky with their binoculars, taking it in turns to peer one-eyed through the telescope. They reminded Martin of some impossible incident from the Boer War, soldiers perhaps, receiving intelligence of a distant disaster – or Afghan warriors signalling the advance of the infidel with burnished mirrors. Bringing the news from Ghent to Aix. He was surprised at himself, for he was not normally subject to such flights of fancy. He wondered if the altitude was getting to him.

Or was it simply that his outlook had begun to change during his brief sojourn in the land of the lion? Not so long ago the idea of receiving cricketing news by carrier pigeon would have seemed ludicrous to Martin. As absurd as keeping tarantulas in a pencil box or sacrificing a goat. Now it seemed eminently logical, as did so much else in this extraordinary environment. His eyes were being opened to a new world, far removed from the comfortable, ordered domesticity of Purley Way. A world he did not necessarily approve of, but which held him fascinated in its grip.

It was nearly tea time before the next message arrived. '*St Brendan's 38 for 3. Both openers gone.*'

Five minutes later they were 41 for 5.

'I don't like the sound of that,' Desmond commented. 'Too many wickets in hand.'

A lull followed which lasted almost until dark. The enthusiasts dwindled, slipping away one by one until only a handful of diehards remained. A bell rang for the evening meal; another for prep. The sun disappeared behind the Mau escarpment, throwing the world into shadow; and with it, against the last of the day, the urgent flutter of wings.

'*St Brendan's 46 for 7. Three overs left.*' The Padre's writing was hurried, as if he could not tear his eyes from the game.

'Three overs,' said Martin. 'That means we should have a result soon.'

They waited. No more messages came. The boys went up to the dormitories and prepared for sleep. Martin stayed in the pigeon loft with a flashlamp, ready to pass the word as soon as it arrived. Lights out was delayed fifteen minutes, the boys sat up in bed. Still no result.

'I can't understand it,' Desmond said. 'The game finished three hours ago. Those birds ought to have been here by now.'

'Something's happened.' Martin scanned the sky. 'They must have got lost on the way.'

Lights out. The boys in darkness, resigned to a shallow sleep. In the loft, Martin flashed his torch over the boxes one last time. No new birds had returned to the nest, none had been mistakenly overlooked in the gloom. There was no point waiting any longer, the game had been over too long. He decided to call it a day.

Half an hour later, headlights along the drive and the raucous sound of singing:

> *There were rats, rats, wearing colonels' hats,*
> *In the stores, in the stores . . .'*

'That sounds like them,' said Desmond.

> *'. . . in the Quartermaster's stores.*
> *My eyes are dim, I cannot see,*
> *I have not brought my specs with me . . .'*

The bus pulled up at the front door. First out was the Padre.

'There you are, headmaster.' He sounded jubilant.

'Padre, you've been drinking!'

'Only a small one. We stopped off at Nakuru. The Stag's Head. I thought a little celebration was in order.'

'You won then?'

'Won?' The Padre had been thinking of Father Heffernan. 'Certainly we won. By three runs in the last over. A brilliant match, headmaster – all down to Nightshade and Fife-Nugent. We must give them their colours.'

'The last we heard was 46 for 7.'

'Which means . . .' the Padre grasped the point '. . . that Siege of Paris isn't back. Blast! I knew it was going to be close, so I saved him till the end. I was hoping he'd have been here long ago.'

'There's no sign of him in the loft,' said Martin. 'I checked.'

'Perhaps he'll turn up tomorrow, Padre.'

'He must. Wretched bird! I'm depending on him. He's the best I've got for breeding purposes.'

25

But although the Padre rose with the dawn, nursing an aching head, there was still no sign of Siege of Paris. His nesting box was empty, his corn untouched. He had not returned to the loft all night.

Daylight brought an aeroplane instead – a four seater, indistinguishable at first from the vultures wheeling speculatively across the plain. It came from the Aberdares, losing height rapidly, and landed with a bump at the far end of the playing fields.

An elderly settler got out, a choleric-looking man, followed by a woman who was obviously his wife. Behind them, pale and reluctant, came Smith-Baggot.

'We found him in the barn at home,' explained his father. 'Been there some time apparently. We were wondering why the dogs were barking. We're bringing him back now for one last chance.'

Smith-Baggot looked embarrassed, as well he might. 'What a lot of trouble you've caused,' Desmond told him. 'Go straight to my study and wait for me there. Nodleman, see that he does. I shall deal with him later.'

Eugene led Smith-Baggot away. The others discussed schools.

'Eton appears to be out,' observed Smith-Baggot père. 'Though why that should be, I don't know. The Smith-Baggots have always gone to Eton.'

'Maths was the trouble,' the Padre explained. 'And English. And history.'

'We've put him down for a spread of places. Marlborough, Rugby, Lancing – it all depends where we can get him in.'

'Not Rugby, darling,' pleaded Mrs Smith-Baggot. 'Shopkeepers' sons.'

'Or Charterhouse. What do you think of Charterhouse?'

'Tricky,' said Desmond.

'We want him to take the common entrance again next term. We don't care where, just so long as it's somewhere.'

'Have you ever considered King's, Canterbury?'

'King's, Canterbury?' Mr Smith-Baggot was suspicious. 'What sort of place is that?'

'All beer and rugby, I'm afraid. Second Division. But useful in cases like this.'

'Think they'd take him?'

'Nothing is ever certain.' Desmond hedged his bet. 'With special pleading perhaps. They like a percentage of colonials.'

'Oh well. If they like colonials. . . .'

So, more or less by default, it was arranged that Smith-Baggot should sit the common entrance next term to the King's School, Canterbury. His parents climbed back into their aircraft, studying the prospectus, and flew home. Desmond waved them off and went to beat their son for running away.

'Four,' he announced, chalking the cane. 'It would have been more, only your father's already thrashed you once at home.'

'Thank you very much, sir.'

It had also been agreed that Smith-Baggot would need extra tuition during the weeks that followed to have any hope of passing. Eugene, who was short of money, volunteered for the task.

'I don't know,' Desmond said doubtfully. 'They'd be alone together all day. He's all right, is he, Nodleman? He isn't. . . ?'

'He has a wife who researches in Connecticut, headmaster. A Ms Himmelfarb. They see each other every summer.'

'All the same, Padre, I think you'd better do it. You can never trust Americans to teach history correctly.'

'I shall need help.'

'You can have Riddle. He knows the form. Get him onto it straight away.'

Martin and the Padre shared the job between them. They left

125

Eugene to complete his thesis and took Smith-Baggot under their wing, drawing up a comprehensive revision programme to pinpoint his various weaknesses. Martin taught maths and algebra, the Padre English and history. Once a week for the rest of term they also coached him in the finer points of exam technique, a subject in which he was notably deficient. They found it an uphill struggle at first, for Smith-Baggot was an unresponsive pupil. He was thinner after his time on the mountain, improperly nourished, unable to prevent his mind from wandering. He had fallen foul of a tapeworm, a legacy of the biltong he had consumed.

'Raw meat, you see,' the Padre told him. 'You should never eat meat without cooking it first.'

Mrs Fist did what she could, but for a long time the tapeworm defied her best efforts at removal. She tried all sorts of remedies without success. The tapeworm grew by leaps and bounds, clinging to the wall of Smith-Baggot's stomach, rebuffing all attempts to dislodge it.

'I don't know what to do with him,' she admitted at last. 'I honestly don't. I've tried everything it says in the book, but I still can't get rid of the bloody thing.'

'Johnson's easy-worm for dogs.' Lady Bullivant was triumphant. 'You should have told me before. It never fails.'

Before Mrs Fist could stop her, Lady Bullivant got hold of Smith-Baggot and dosed him. She was right: the pills cured him within days. But the odium remained. It was rumoured in the changing room that anyone who touched him – or allowed him to touch them – would fall prey to all manner of loathsome disease.

'Watch out for his towel,' Nightshade warned the others one day. 'You can see the rabies from here.'

'Leprosy,' insisted Fife-Nugent. 'All scabs and slime.'

'And gonorrhoea,' said Karanja. 'And pus.'

'Fuck off,' Smith-Baggot told them.

He retreated to the latrines. The others followed. There were no doors on the cubicles, a precaution against suicide or worse. But at least he could not be attacked from behind. He found a vacant seat and defiantly plumped himself down, his trousers around his ankles. The others crowded in after him.

126

'Jesus, what a stink!'

'Like a munt.'

Smith-Baggot stuck silently to his seat. Even in the latrines, there could be no relief. The others continued to torment him for a while, then became bored. They turned and shuffled out of the cubicle, pausing only to remove all the lavatory paper so that Smith-Baggot was left with none for his own use. He remained where he was, certain of further trouble if he tried to emerge. Settling down on the seat, he rested his head in his hands and resigned himself to a lengthy wait before the all clear.

He was still waiting when the police came to arrest Mogadishu.

26

They arrested him on charges of arson and attempted murder. He was guilty by his own admission. He had been heard in Naivasha, boasting of how he had set fire to the Catholic mission and dispersed the white fathers. He did not deny the charge. He expected to be congratulated instead.

'I'll never understand Africans,' said Desmond. 'As long as I live, I'll never know what makes them tick.' He gestured helplessly. 'I always thought I knew Mogadishu pretty well, but I never would have guessed he'd do anything like this. It just doesn't make sense.'

'We must get him back,' said the Padre. 'He's the only one who knows how to roll the pitch properly.'

'They're like women. You think you know them, you think you understand them, but sooner or later they always do something totally incomprehensible – and you realise you have no point of contact at all.'

'The police, headmaster. You must go down and see the inspector, find out what's at the bottom of it. Mogadishu must have had a motive of some kind. We must find out what.'

Desmond was back within two hours. He sent at once for Martin.

'It's your fault,' he accused. 'You put Mogadishu up to it.'

'I did?'

'I saw Mogadishu. He explained everything. How you told him it was all right to set fire to Catholics. They do it all the time in England, you said. Mogadishu was most particular about that. Bwana Riddle saying it was okay.'

Martin sat down. 'Oh dear,' he said.

'I should think so! Inciting the coons to murder! What on earth were you playing at?'

Martin explained about Guy Fawkes. Desmond listened impatiently.

'That's no excuse. You should have known better. They're children, these people. You can't treat them like rational human beings. You always have to watch what you say.'

Martin apologised.

'Yes yes.' Desmond waved a hand. 'The question is, what are we going to do about it? We've got to get Mogadishu off the hook somehow. We can't just leave him in the nick.'

'Oh dear.'

'And for Christ's sake stop saying Oh dear!'

27

'Oh Christ,' said Martin.

He burned with shame. He wondered what he could do to retrieve the situation.

'Perhaps I should go and see the police?' he suggested. 'Explain that it was all a terrible mistake.'

'You could do.' Desmond had little faith in Martin's powers of persuasion. 'I don't suppose it would do any harm.'

'I'd like to try.'

'All right then.' Desmond was glad to be rid of him. He tossed over a set of keys. 'Take the Landrover and get on down to Naivasha. The inspector's a reasonable type. He might at least let you see Mogadishu while you're there.'

Martin shrank from the keys. He writhed inwardly. He had a further indignity to confess.

'I can't drive,' he said.

'You can't drive?'

Martin hung his head. Desmond took a deep breath, got up and looked out of the window. He saw Nightshade with a pot of treacle, attempting to divert a column of safari ants through the open door of the staff room.

'Nightshade, are you doing anything?'

'Me sir? No sir.' Nightshade hid the treacle behind his back.

'Well you should be, you idle sod. Take these keys and drive Mr Riddle in to Naivasha.'

'Wouldn't Mr Riddle like to drive himself, sir?'

'Mr Riddle *doesn't know how.*'

'But surely . . .?' objected Martin. 'Nightshade's only twelve. Surely he can't . . . .'

130

'This is frontier country.' Desmond didn't bother to hide his contempt. 'Everyone learns at twelve.'

So Nightshade drove to the police station, with Martin in deep humiliation beside him. Nightshade was the average size for his age, but still could barely see over the dashboard. He drove easily, one hand on his knee, with a skill learned on up-country roads.

'It's simple, once you know how,' he told Martin. 'You can have a go on the way back, if you like.'

They arrived at the station. The police inspector was sympathetic to their cause; Mogadishu less so. He was polite, but distinctly aggrieved. One eye was closed where the police had beaten him, and he walked with a slight limp. Martin spent an uncomfortable half hour in the cells with him, attempting to explain that the burning of Guy Fawkes had been an isolated incident, that Roman Catholics in England were not by and large tied to the stake. Setting fire to the mission, he pointed out, was not what happened in England at all. Mogadishu listened courteously, but without comprehension, making little secret of the injury he felt he had been done. Martin's explanation did nothing to set his mind at rest.

The police inspector offered little comfort either. Mogadishu would have to go to Nairobi for trial, he said. There was nothing he could do about it. Not unless Martin could suggest a way round the problem. The police inspector rubbed his thumb and forefinger together as he spoke; but Martin, who was still unfamiliar with the ways of the world, attached no significance to this.

That night the leopard returned to Haggard Hall. Its victim this time was human. Mogadishu's *toto*.

'You could hear the bones crunching apparently,' said Desmond. 'And we found the body too. What was left of it. We must have disturbed him while he was still feeding.'

'Dose it with strychnine,' advised Lady Bullivant. 'That leopard's bound to come back.'

'I don't know. It seems a bit hard. Mogadishu was very fond of the child.'

'One *toto* more or less makes no difference. Mogadishu would only have left it out for the hyenas anyway.'

So the remains of the *toto* were sprinkled with strychnine and laid out invitingly on a path close to the leopard's last known whereabouts. Two pi-dogs found them soon afterwards and were in turn found next day, stiff with rigor mortis. The leopard was a wily animal. It changed hunting grounds until the fuss died down and was not heard of again until two nights before the end of term. Then it ate Lady Bullivant's dog Mugabe.

'This is too much,' she grieved. 'I *said* something would have to be done.'

She did it herself. Sending for the game warden, she conscripted all the servants in the neighbourhood and organized them into a motley array of beaters armed with pots, pans and streamers of coloured cloth. Some two hundred natives under her command were herded towards the forest's edge, where Lady Bullivant appeared on horseback to lead them into battle.

'We go forward in extended line,' she told the game warden, 'until we flush the bugger out. We'll force him up towards the open ground. Then you bag him with your gun.'

The warden passed the plan on to the natives. They expressed doubts.

'They're worried the leopard might double back and go for one of them.'

'Nonsense. Tell them to push on.'

Reluctantly, the natives complied. At five yard intervals, dragging their feet, they advanced nervously into the forest and began to beat their drums. One or two made as if to turn back, but were dissuaded by the sight of Lady Bullivant, who had positioned herself in the rear to deter stragglers. The rest chose the lesser of two evils and pressed forward.

Before long, the leopard was cornered. It broke cover as predicted and was brought down by the warden with a hypodermic dart. Martin, who was among the beaters, arrived just in time to see it sink to its knees, shaking its head dizzily as it fought to stay awake. From one flank protruded the offending dart. A few yards further on, the warden was crouched over his rifle, waiting cautiously for the drug to take effect.

'Good oh.' Lady Bullivant dismounted and prodded the slumbering animal with her boot. It offered no resistance. From her saddlebag she produced a poker, a fearsome implement, wrapped in cloth around the handle. 'Now all we need is a fire,' she declared.

Soon smoke was rising. Lady Bullivant plunged the poker into the flames and watched over it until the tip began to glow red hot. Then, holding it by the cloth, she advanced purposefully on the leopard's anus.

'What are you up to with that?' demanded the warden.

'I don't want to mark the pelt.' She lifted its tail. 'No point ruining a perfectly good skin.'

'You're not going to kill it with a poker!'

'Now look here, young man . . . .'

But the warden was impertinent as well as young. Despite Lady Bullivant's protestations, he saw to it that the animal was packed into a wooden crate instead and carted off to the Aberdares to be set free in the national park. Martin watched it go. It was awoken some hours later, in a totally new environment, by the time honoured expedient of getting an African to bite it at the root of the tail.

28

This was little comfort to Lady Bullivant. Without Mugabe, she was left with only Nkomo for company. She kept him close to her, in case the leopard had a mate, and sought consolation for her bereavement in a flurry of activity, beginning with a transformation of the stables. During the first week of the holidays she reorganised them from top to bottom, making inventories, drawing up programmes, redesigning the tack room to her own demanding specifications. She let nothing escape her eye. It had long been the custom of the chief syce to reallocate a portion of the horses' feed to his own ever-burgeoning family – a custom that was now summarily discontinued, along with a variety of similar practices. Lady Bullivant produced a lock for the stores and saw to it that feed was distributed only under her personal supervision. As an example to the syce, she also gelded a new pair of stallions in a welter of blood and profanity.

When she had finished the inventory, she wrote out a shopping list for Martin, who was accompanying Desmond to Nairobi for Mogadishu's trial.

'Colic drench, liniment, a sharp draw knife,' she told him. 'Hoof rasp, pincers, blunt-ended scissors. Sulphamide if you can find any. And electrolytes for the water. Horses dehydrate without them.'

'Right ho.'

'Don't let them cheat you. Tell them you're doing it for me.'

Mrs Fist had a list too, for a trip to Nairobi was a rare event.

'Tights, Tampax, mascara. Cigarettes if you can get them, Martin. And something to read – anything from Mills and Boon.'

'What that woman wants stockings for, I don't know,' sniffed Lady Bullivant.

134

The supplies of Gentleman's Relish were holding out, so the Padre had no list. But Eugene had a favour to ask.

'Will you mail this for me?' He handed over a bulky object in a recycled jiffy bag. 'It's my book. A couple of specimen chapters. I want it recorded delivery.'

The manuscript was addressed to a New York publisher. It contained everything Eugene had discovered about the Masai. With it went all his hopes and fears for the future.

'I'll see what I can do,' Martin promised.

He popped the manuscript into the Landrover and slipped gingerly behind the wheel. A homemade L plate front and rear indicated that he was going to do the driving. The episode with Nightshade had caught him on a raw nerve.

Desmond sat unwillingly in the passenger seat, arms across his chest. 'Start off in neutral,' he advised gruffly. 'Check your rear mirror before you move out.'

Martin did as he was told and stepped on the accelerator. A cloud of dust arose, accompanied by a high pitched whine. Desmond braced his legs. Martin experimented hastily and came by chance to the handbrake. The vehicle rocketed forward.

They had gone two miles before Desmond could stand no more. 'Move over,' he ordered. 'I'll drive.'

Martin was glad to oblige. Driving was more difficult than it looked. He changed places with a sigh of relief, delighted to be a passenger once more. Desmond took the wheel and did not relinquish it again until they reached Nairobi.

'Drop off your bag at the Norfolk,' he told Martin when they arrived. 'You can stay there tonight. I'll be at the Muthaiga Club if you need me.'

Muthaiga was where the old hands stayed. 'Wouldn't it be better if I went with you?' Martin asked wistfully.

'Lord, no.' Desmond's club was hallowed ground. 'The Norfolk'll do fine. You'll find it very comfortable.'

So Martin dropped his case at the Norfolk. Desmond waited at the veranda while he went to check in. The veranda was packed with tourists, for the Norfolk was Kenya's most famous hotel — host in its day to Roosevelt and Churchill, Hemingway and Edward

VIII. Clark Gable had dined on the veranda with Grace Kelly; Stewart Granger with Deborah Kerr. Lord Delamere had shot all the bottles off the bar-room counter; Lord Erroll had rogered women on the billiard table during his lunch hour. The Norfolk's was an eclectic history, a reflection of the community it served.

The tourists watched Martin with mild curiosity. They were Americans mostly, with a sprinkling of Europeans, pale in the sunlight, obviously out of place. One or two, Martin noticed wryly, wore bush hats of synthetic leopardskin. He was pleased that his own clothes, bought up-country, marked him out as one of the locals, someone who indubitably knew his way around.

'*Toa hii*,' he told a porter, pointing to his suitcase. '*Nataka kwenda chumba tafadhali.*'

'*Ndio, bwana.*' The porter trotted inside with the case. Martin followed at a more dignified speed. He was conscious of a linguistic coup the onlookers could not hope to emulate.

When he came out again, Desmond drove him on to the Law Courts, an old colonial building dwarfed now by the skyscrapers of a more brutal age. Mogadishu's trial was scheduled for the afternoon, an open and shut case, provisionally expected to be over at one sitting. Witnesses had been gathering for it since mid-morning. The first person they saw as they entered was Father Heffernan, whispering conspiratorially in the corridor with a trio of altar boys. Mogadishu's native chums waited uneasily in another corner – they were witnesses for the prosecution. The police inspector from Naivasha nodded distantly to Martin and patrolled up and down, jangling his keys. In his top pocket was a confession signed by the accused with an X. Of Mogadishu himself there was no sign. He was still in the cells.

The case was to be tried by three African assessors rather than a jury. A cheerful noise from their robing room, just behind the urinals, testified to a good lunch as they prepared to send Mogadishu down for five years.

'You hold the fort here,' Desmond told Martin. 'I've got to have a pee. I shan't be a minute.'

He was five. When he returned, the doors had opened and the court was in session.

First to give evidence was Father Heffernan. Father Heffernan was a humourless-looking man with a fringe of hair over an ascetic forehead. He took the stand and spoke eloquently, with obvious feeling, of the destruction of his mission. Everything had been burned, he told the court. Everything had gone up in flames. Even, inexplicably, his piece of the True Cross, which might have been expected to survive such a conflagration.

He was followed by Mogadishu's chums. They gave evidence shiftily, reluctant to admit to anything, conceding when cornered that they might perhaps have heard the accused boast of destroying the mission – but only under the influence of *khat*. Their story was corroborated by Mogadishu, ill and gaunt after his time in custody, who made no bones about it; and by Martin, his character witness, who shamefacedly admitted his part in the proceedings. As a white man, and a teacher, better things had been expected of him.

To all this the assessors listened sombrely, with faces of graven slate. The issue was cut and dried. Mogadishu stood condemned out of his own mouth, out of the mouths of all who knew him. The assessors retired at three-thirty to consider their judgment. It was obvious to everyone in the courtroom that they would not be out long. Desmond lit a cigarette and settled down to wait.

'I hope they're not too hard on him,' Martin worried.

'We'll know soon enough.' Desmond blew a smoke ring.

The assessors returned. One by one they took their places on the bench. At a command from the warders, Mogadishu was brought forward to hear his sentence. The senior assessor produced a pair of spectacles with a somewhat theatrical gesture and announced the verdict. Not Guilty.

'It seems an odd decision when you think about it,' said Martin, as the three of them drove home. 'You'd have expected him to be guilty really, with all that evidence against him.'

Desmond patted his wallet. 'I fixed the judges. A month each out of your salary. Africa, Riddle. You've got to learn. It's a different world.'

29

So ended Martin's first term of schoolmastering in Kenya, a term without precedence in his experience. Arson, dismemberment, sudden death – there had been more excitement during his few weeks at Haggard Hall than in all his previous life at Purley Way. He was pleased, after a fashion. This was clearly what the army had meant by getting his knees brown.

He wondered what his parents would have said if they could see him now, in the heart of darkness, speaking the lingo like a native, visiting murderers in the cells – driving almost. Now that he thought about it, he had not been in touch with his parents for a long time, scarcely at all since his arrival at Haggard Hall. Odd really, when you considered what an attentive son he had been in the past. Always ready to help with the shopping, to accompany his mother on the bus. Odd that his life should have changed so dramatically, virtually without his realising it. Gone was the Martin of yesterday, the shy physicist, honorary secretary of the college gramophone society. Gone the young man who had frozen all evening in his room rather than attend the freshers' dance. Well, almost gone. The events of the past couple of months had seen to that.

Would they recognise him still, those dancing freshers, those confident public schoolboys of Red Group? Martin rather thought not. He felt that he had changed since his arrival in Africa, had blossomed in a myriad of ways. True there had been the hat, the Sainsbury's bag, the business with Mogadishu – Martin still squirmed at the memory. But that was all behind him now. He would not make the same mistakes again. He was learning fast, fast enough to contemplate the future without misgiving. Or so he told himself.

Two letters arrived for him in what remained of the holidays. Both reminded him of home. The first was from his mother, chiding him for not writing more often: *'What have you been doing with yourself, Martin, you haven't told us? Dad and I spent Christmas here as usual with Gran, but it wasn't the same without you. We watched Morecambe and Wise on Boxing Day, remember how they used to make you laugh!! There hasn't been any snow yet, you never know we're keeping our fingers crossed, the weather man says we might have some before long. Must catch the post now. Lots of love and write soon, you haven't for ages. You're very naughty. Mrs Simmonds sends her best. Mum XXX.'*

The other arrived just before the start of the new term. It was from the army, naming the date for his return to the Regular Commissions Board.

PART TWO

The Masai

1

'I always hate the beginning of term.' Desmond could not conceal his gloom. 'So much to do, so many people to see. There's never a moment to one's self.'

'Mrs Fife-Nugent is here, headmaster. Something to do with his last report.'

'*Weight, beginning of term: 6 stone 3. End of term: 5 stone 10.* I *knew* she wouldn't like that.'

It was mid-afternoon in Desmond's study. The school had been trickling back since lunch. Outside the window a new boy was in tears, consoled by a grieving mother.

'God how I loathe them!' Desmond went on. 'Why do they bother to come if they're only going to snivel?'

Mrs Fist put her head in. 'Smith-Baggot's back. His parents wanted you to know.'

'Are they still here?'

'I think so.'

'Don't let them near me.'

Mothers, fathers, brothers, sisters; the corridor full of alien voices. It had been a good holiday for the staff. Eugene had completed the bulk of his thesis, Desmond had fished for trout, Mogadishu had been reconciled with his wife. Now they were at work again.

'Mr Karanja is here too, headmaster. He wants to talk to you about the Romantic poets.'

'You deal with him, Padre. I'll take Mrs Fife-Nugent.'

New beds, new faces, the unpacking of trunks. Tea for parents in the staff room, for boys in the dining hall. Then a series of brittle farewells: the hurried kiss, the slammed car door, the crunch of wheels on gravel.

At four Desmond called the roll. Everyone had returned, everyone except Nightshade. He arrived much later, after dark, with a long story of having been held up by elephants at Molo.

'They wouldn't move, sir. We waited and waited, but they wouldn't get off the road.'

'There are no elephants at Molo, Nightshade.'

'There were, sir. A whole herd.'

The boys went to bed at seven. At five past, Desmond summoned the staff to his room for a meeting. He called it an O group, after his time in the army.

'The main thing this term is to get rid of Smith-Baggot,' he told them. 'I don't care how we do it, but we've got to make sure he passes the common entrance this time around, no questions asked. Otherwise we shall all be on the spot.'

'Easier said than done, headmaster.'

'Quite so, Padre. But he's got to go. You know that as well as I do.'

'He'll have to work harder on his maths,' Martin warned.

'And his English, and his history. He'll have to work harder on everything. In a hurry too. That's why we must all rally round.'

Everyone rallied. Even, in his way, Smith-Baggot. He had not enjoyed the recent holiday as much as he might have done. It had not been the change from school that he had been hoping for. The common entrance had loomed large in the conversation of the household, larger even than rinderpest or the possibility of drought. The common entrance for three meals a day; morning, noon and night. There had been no let-up for Smith-Baggot in his own home, no respite. First one parent, then the other, then both together had been at him with dire warnings as to his future, dire predictions as to what would happen if he were to find himself in a few months, public school-less of public school age. The idea did not bear thinking about.

All of which contributed to a creeping paralysis of mind which overcame him as the term progressed and effectively prevented him from learning anything new. His brain persistently refused to function. There were only two candidates for the exam that term, himself and Karanja, comfortably certain of passing first time to Wellington. Two candidates with a mountain of stuff to learn – tans, cosines, square roots; the Norman Invasion, the Black Death; genitive, dative, subjunctive; French irregular verbs, the difference between grave and acute, the nouns that take x in the plural. A mountain of stuff, the majority of it incomprehensible. Smith-Baggot made progress, but there was a limit to how much he could hoist in.

A week before the first exam, the Padre tested him on history. The result was not encouraging.

'1170, Smith-Baggot. What happened in 1170?'

'Magna Carta, sir?'

'The murder of Thomas à Becket. Can you tell me where he was murdered? No? Canterbury, Smith-Baggot. In the middle of the Cathedral.'

'A Cathedral, sir? At Canterbury?'

'It's going to be touch and go,' the Padre reported to Desmond. 'We can't afford to let up for a *moment*.'

2

Two days later the syce delivered a saddlebag of mail to the staff room. It contained the question papers, air mail from England. They came in a brown paper parcel, carefully sealed, and were taken under escort to Desmond's study. He locked them in a drawer and, mindful of Smith-Baggot's previous escapade, pocketed the key.

'I shall sit up every night with a shotgun,' he warned. 'Those papers will be *quite* safe where they are.'

The saddlebag also contained a letter for Eugene. It came from New York and was overstamped '*Hi there, mailperson, have a nice day*!'

'What sort of a place *is* America?' Desmond wondered.

Eugene tore the letter open. His fingers were unaccountably trembling.

'It's from the publishers,' he announced after an interval. 'They like it. They like my book.'

The publishers enclosed the reader's report on the specimen chapters Eugene had submitted during the vacation. The report was full of praise. It compared Eugene to Smetterling Farfala, whose definitive study of the wa-Chagga was famous.

'We shall all want a signed copy,' said Lady Bullivant.

Eugene read on. 'They're wondering about a TV series. They think they can sell it to the networks.'

'A series about what?'

'My life among the Masai. The only white man ever to become a blood brother. They want it to be the book of the film.'

A stunned silenced followed.

'I suppose there'll be money in it?' Desmond asked in disbelief.

'You're not kidding! A TV tie-in is a gold mine. I shall have to get an agent.'

'About your life among the Masai?' Martin was puzzled. 'But surely. . . ?'

'Maybe two agents. One for the west coast. That's where the deals are tied up.'

'A blood brother?'

'As good as.' Eugene was studying his contract. 'It's simply a formality.'

He was elated. His career, lately a source of concern to him, was looking up. Whatever else might happen, there would plainly be tenure in this.

'It's made for television,' he pointed out. 'It's got everything. Wild life, scenery, ethnicity. A great story line – one man's struggle against the forces of nature. They love that kind of thing in Milwaukee.'

'A *blood* brother!'

'Why not? They trust me, after all. I'm their friend.'

3

Euphoria for Eugene; but not for Smith-Baggot. He had little enough to be happy about. At ten-to-nine on the morning of the first exam, all feeling had gone from his legs and he could think of nothing except the unpleasantness that lay ahead. The death wish hung over him like a shroud. He had been awake since five, worrying about his future.

Reluctantly he presented himself at the staff room door. So did Karanja. Each carried pen, pencil, rubber, a bottle of ink, a supply of geometrical instruments. Each was impatient for the ordeal to begin.

'All set?' inquired the Padre.

Smith-Baggot nodded dumbly. All was as set as ever it would be. Whatever happened now was out of his hands.

Martin invigilated. He sat at the master's table, writing to the Regular Commissions Board, while the two candidates scanned the upturned papers. The first exam was English, a soft option to start with. Grammar, composition, spelling; an essay on one of the following subjects – food, pets, going for a walk. The candidates scribbled busily.

'How was it?' Desmond asked at lunch.

'All right. Karanja seemed okay, but I'm not so sure about Smith-Baggot. He didn't know what paraphrase meant.'

After English, geography. Then maths and French, then the rest. Where is Ben Nevis; what is the supine of *confiteor*; why are the triangles ABC and XYZ congruent; how did Sir Francis Drake singe the King of Spain's beard? When, where, why, who? Three and a half days of exams, three and a half days to single out sheep from goats, tomorrow's leaders from tomorrow's also ran.

Smith-Baggot handed in his papers to Desmond at the end. He

148

was not optimistic. Neither was Desmond. They knew, both of them, that if anybody was going to be an also ran, it would be Smith-Baggot.

The papers provided ample confirmation.

'Look at this, for God's sake! *The Glorious Revolution happened in 1866 when King James dropped his seal in the Thames.*'

'Along the right lines, headmaster.'

'That date will have to come out.'

'Not strictly ethical, headmaster.'

'A slip of the pen. Smith-Baggot needn't be penalised for that.' Desmond skilfully amended it. 'What about this! *Tundra grows in the tropics.* You know what I think, Padre? We're going to have to give him some help.'

'What sort of help?'

'A few alterations here and there. Nothing spectacular. Enough to make up for his absence from school.'

'Headmaster, we couldn't possibly do that.'

'Not even one or two?'

'Not even one or two.'

'Of course not, Padre. It was just an idle thought.'

What the eye doesn't see, the heart doesn't grieve over. Desmond was missing from tea that day. A backlog of paperwork kept him in his study all afternoon. He did not emerge until just before the syce was due to leave for Naivasha with the mail. Without looking at the Padre, he handed over two buff envelopes, one addressed to Wellington, the other to Canterbury. The syce put them in his bag and mounted up. The papers were out of Desmond's hands. Within four days they would reach their respective destinations. A week later, according to the published schedule, the results would be officially declared.

'Now all we can do is wait,' said Desmond.

4

While they waited, Martin went down to Nairobi again and took his driving test. It was his last chance before returning to England.

He took the test more in hope than expectation. Although he had been practising for it daily, he had formed a low – and perfectly accurate – opinion of his own driving, and was not at all sanguine about his prospects. It would be a miracle, he told himself, if ever he passed.

So it proved. He stalled the car in Kenyatta Avenue, forgot to indicate on numerous occasions (or rather did not forget but was reluctant to let go the wheel), and joined a main road at speed because he had found no way of stopping at the T junction. The examiner was not impressed. But Martin left a wad of twenty-shilling notes on the seat between them – as Desmond had advised him to – and came away with a brand new licence, no questions asked.

Feeling rather raffish – he had never attempted to bribe anyone before, let alone successfully – he hired a car with the last of his money and drove himself back to Naivasha. He drove atrociously, but no worse than anyone else. Among the natives there had been a move at independence to celebrate the new freedom by throwing open both sides of the road to traffic, and this policy still had its adherents. Martin arrived safely at Haggard Hall, but more sinned against than sinning.

He went at once to share his good news with the Padre and found him in the pigeon loft, mildly abstracted, deaf to the toot toot of Martin's horn and the ostentatious gunning of his motor. The Padre was not interested in driving tests. He was making the final preparations for Smith-Baggot's results, which were to be delivered to his parents, as before, by carrier pigeon. A young

Dewlap waited in its basket, chafing vigorously amid alien surroundings. In the Padre's opinion, it was not up to the task in hand.

'If I only had another one like Siege of Paris,' he complained. 'He'd have been just the job for the Smith-Baggots.'

'I passed my test,' said Martin.

'Did you? I'm sure you did. It goes to show, doesn't it?' If I hadn't taken Paris to St Brendan's, I could have bred from him by now. I could have had all the Sieges I wanted, if only I'd thought.'

The railway line that brought the mail from Nairobi could just be discerned from the loft with binoculars, curving slowly across the floor of the valley. On the day the results were due, the Padre set Karanja and Smith-Baggot to keep a watch for it. They reported half an hour early, inwardly steeling themselves, and took it in turns to balance on the guard rail, straining for a first glimpse of the train. They were on edge in more ways than one, for the moment of truth was near.

'What can you see?' Karanja demanded.

'Nothing.'

'You must be able to see something.'

'I told you. Nothing.'

The train was late. This was not an unusual occurrence, but today it seemed particularly irksome. The two boys began to fret.

'Maybe it's been delayed.'

'Maybe it's hit a rhino on the line.'

'Maybe it came and we missed it.'

The argument was settled by the appearance of the engine around the side of Longonot. Followed by two pairs of eyes it crawled across the plain, barely visible at the distance, and pulled in to the twinkling rooftops of Naivasha.

'It's there, sir!' Karanja yelled. 'It's arrived!'

'Give it half an hour,' answered the Padre, 'then we'll go and collect the mail.'

'Longer,' said Desmond. 'They're an idle bunch at the post office.'

151

Smith-Baggot said nothing. He could find no words for the misery in his stomach.

The time passed slowly. Desmond had decided to collect the mail in person; anticipating good news from Wellington, he wanted to use the phone at the post office to try and ring Karanja's father. Martin volunteered to go with him: he was anxious to speak to Desmond privately. The Padre retreated to the pigeon loft and wrote out two messages for the Smith-Baggots, one bearing good news, the other bad.

'Not long now,' he told Smith-Baggot.

'That's what I'm afraid of, sir.'

Desmond started the car. Martin joined him in the passenger seat. They drove along the lake road, through a herd of Thomson's gazelle grazing illicitly at the edge of the papyrus. A fish eagle hung mutely on the warm air, behind it a pair of pelicans. The umbrella trees formed a broad swathe of yellow against the blue depths of the water.

'I was thinking of going back to England next week,' Martin said diffidently.

'Were you?'

'If you don't need me any more. The army wants to see me again.'

'I shouldn't keep them waiting.'

Martin ducked his head in acknowledgement. It was now or never for the army, he was certain of that. His time in Africa had been a revelation to him, an object lesson in everything the Regular Commissions Board held dear. What mattered now was to go home and show them what he had learned.

Naivasha appeared immune to the arrival of the morning train. No traffic moved, nothing stirred. The dust thrown up by Desmond's wheels swirled across the street, choking the *dukas* with fumes, and settled unnoticed on a trio of old men outside the beer hall.

Desmond parked in front of the post office and led the way inside. An old Somali woman was squatting across the threshold with a child at each breast. Desmond and Martin stepped over her. The mail was kept in a row of green metal boxes, each with its

152

own key. Desmond unlocked the school's box and opened the door. He pulled out a sheaf of letters and sorted quickly through them until he found what he was looking for.

'Karanja's in,' he announced.

'What about Smith-Baggot?'

Desmond searched further. He unearthed a white envelope with '*If undelivered, please return to The King's School, Canterbury*' on it in bold type.

'Here we are,' he said.

He scanned the letter and flipped it across to Martin.

'That's it then,' said Martin.

Half an hour later, the Padre emerged from the loft and launched a tiny grey pigeon into the sky. Round its leg was the message the Smith-Baggots had been waiting for: '*CONGRATULATIONS PASSED CE*'.

But Smith-Baggot knew nothing of this. He had run away again.

5

'God damn his eyes! God damn him to hell!' Desmond was losing patience with Smith-Baggot.

He had gone south this time, towards Mount Longonot. He was not carrying any food or water. It had been a spur of the moment decision to run away, a decision born of desperation.

'We can get him back if we hurry,' said the Padre. 'Shall I arrange air support?'

'Certainly not. His parents won't stand for another bill. We'll have to catch him by ourselves.'

Longonot was a different proposition to the Aberdares. No trees, hardly any cover. A lava-strewn slope rising three thousand feet out of the surrounding plain. Anything moving on it could be seen for miles.

'The usual procedure,' Desmond announced. 'Lady Bullivant can take the right flank on horseback, Nodleman the left. Riddle and the Ndorobo will follow the trail on foot. I shall drive the back-up vehicle with Mogadishu.'

'Uh . . . I'm not really into horses,' Eugene told Lady Bullivant.

'Nonsense. Everyone rides in America.'

They saddled up. Desmond threw a rifle into the back of the Landrover and a couple of *debes*. Martin and the Ndorobo had already set off, tracking their quarry across the veld. Mogadishu packed his spear. At the last minute the Padre appeared with a pair of carrier pigeons for the Landrover.

'You never know when you may need them,' he said.

The rest of the column set out, Lady Bullivant in the lead with Nkomo at her stirrups. She cantered briskly towards the west, intending to cut off Smith-Baggot's line of escape around the side of the volcano. Eugene cantered rather less purposefully towards

154

the east on the same errand. He was not happy on horseback. He came from New England, a world away from Marlboro Country. He rode now purely for the honour of his people.

Desmond brought up the rear in the Landrover – an A Echelon vehicle in military parlance, carrying resupplies for the troops in the field. It was equipped with a medicine chest, a haversack of emergency rations, a kerosene lamp and a blanket. Also a supply of old sacks and a spade for digging out.

He caught up with Martin and the Ndorobo at the foot of the mountain. There was no sign of their quarry. The Ndorobo was on his haunches, examining the ground for clues.

'Marvellous the way these chaps can read the trail, Riddle. Clear as day, when you and I can't see a blind thing.'

The Ndorobo, who had no more idea of Smith-Baggot's whereabouts than anyone else, took a wild guess and pointed upwards with his spear.

'*Juu*,' he gambled. '*Bwana kidogo kwenda juu.*'

'I'll never get the wagon up there.' Desmond shielded his eyes against the sun. 'Plays hell with the suspension. You two will have to struggle on as best you can. You'll get a good view from the top. I'll stay here in case he tries to double back.'

Three thousand feet later Martin did indeed get a good view, his first, of the kingdom of Ayesha, the volcanic bowl spread out far below, its rim so narrow in places that a man could sit astride it with a drop at either foot. It was a view unknown to Rider Haggard, unknown even to Ursula Andress. A view from the gods. But it meant little to Martin, hurrying along in pursuit of Smith-Baggot. Up there, almost in the clouds, his clothes tugged by the wind, he had lost contact with Desmond, had lost contact with everybody except the Ndorobo trotting wordlessly by his side. He was the one with the tracker. He had an uneasy feeling, although they were out of sight, that the others were all depending on him to run their target to earth.

There was still no sign of Smith-Baggot. The tracker cast about as best he could, but without result. As far as the eye could see, in every direction, nothing moved. If Smith-Baggot was there, he was already lying low.

They continued along the lip of the volcano for a mile or so, until they reached the southern extremity, overlooking the Kedong valley. The Kedong was Masai country; Eugene's country. Here he had recorded his lion dance and watched the young warriors eating meat. A small flicker of dust in the east indicated his imminent arrival, bow legged after a tortuous circumnavigation of the mountain. He was followed at a distance by Desmond, bumping across country, who had grown bored of waiting on his own. Towards the west, Lady Bullivant had already established a rallying point and was mounting a lookout from the shade of a thorn tree. Martin and the Ndorobo scrabbled down to join them.

It was obvious from their faces that nobody had seen Smith-Baggot.

'What now?' Eugene demanded.

'When I was hunting Mau Mau,' Desmond remembered, 'we used to shout at them from aeroplanes. A surrender message on a loudspeaker.'

'What did you shout?'

'Oh . . . *Come in, lads, your time is up.* That sort of thing. We only had six seconds, while the plane was overhead.'

'You want us to shout *Come in, Smith-Baggot, you have passed your common entrance?*'

It seemed an unlikely idea.

'We'll get on down to the Masai,' Desmond decided. 'They'll know. If he's been this way, they'll have seen him.'

The column rearranged itself. Martin rode in the Landrover this time, with Mogadishu and the Ndorobo in the back. Desmond was dubious about the extra weight.

'I'm worried about the axle over these potholes. I had one or two nasty bumps coming over.'

But the axle held. Nkomo jumped into the back with the others and panted heavily over Martin's shoulder. It was a fine afternoon. There was little game about at this time of day, but they could see one or two zebra and a single giraffe grazing abstractedly next to a wire fence. Also their first Masai, a group of young men in black togas who emerged from the bush and saluted them with upraised

156

sticks. The young men wore the *isurutia* and were clearly in good humour.

'Youths,' said Eugene. 'Newly circumcised. They're celebrating their coming of age.'

The youths had not seen Smith-Baggot. Nor had a pair of seven-year-olds, tending a herd of cattle. Nor the inhabitants of the first village they came to, a flat-topped *engang* of huts liberally plastered with cow dung.

'That's where they spat on me,' said Eugene.

It was also the site of the famous Kedong massacre, where a Swahili caravan had been wiped out after the caravan leader had abused the hospitality of the Masai by kidnapping two of their women. For years afterwards the ground over a wide area had been strewn with skulls, so many in places that they had been mistaken for ostrich eggs.

'Great days,' said Eugene. 'My friend Ole Sendeyo, the chief *laibon* down here, his pop was on the raid. I may use it in my TV series.'

'You know them well?' Martin asked. 'The people here.'

'I guess. They call me *Naipuroki olowaru*, the black-maned lion. Because of my beard.'

'A bit like Captain Good.'

'Pardon me?'

'Never mind,' said Martin.

They breasted a small rise and came to a stream, barely more than a trickle, that began somewhere on the slopes of Longonot and petered out just as suddenly across the plain. Beyond the stream, about four hundred yards away, a tiny figure trudged unhappily towards the horizon. They looked closer. It was Smith-Baggot.

'There he is!' yelled Desmond. He pressed his foot down.

The Landrover leaped forward. Smith-Baggot spun round, gaped, and vanished into the bundu. Whooping with relief, Desmond jerked the wheel and plunged after him.

Then the axle broke.

6

After Desmond had calmed down, they debated what to do about
it.

'We need to get help,' Eugene pointed out. 'Somebody has to go
to Naivasha for the recovery truck.'

'Too late today.' Lady Bullivant looked at her watch. 'The horses
are dead beat. It would be dark by the time they arrived.'

'We can send a pigeon. The Padre can fix it his end.'

'Even so, nothing can be done today. There isn't enough time.'

'We can't leave the vehicle unattended . . . .'

'We have to stay with it . . . .'

Gradually the idea formed of a night in the bush, with only one
blanket between them.

'When I get hold of Smith-Baggot . . .' said Desmond.

Lady Bullivant looked around. 'There's water in the dip. Plenty
of scrub. We'll build a *boma* for the horses.'

'And a fire. We'll need a fire.'

'And somewhere for the *choo*.'

'I don't know.' Desmond was bitter. He waved a hand at the
empty horizon. 'Sometimes I think I'm getting too old for this
game.'

Reluctantly they set to work. The most urgent priority was to
despatch a pigeon to the Padre, a half-brother to Siege of Paris,
requesting the breakdown truck first thing in the morning. Martin
wrote the message, complete with map reference and compass
bearing. Alone among the party, he was secretly looking forward
to a night under the stars.

Eugene took charge of the *boma*, a thorn fence to keep hyenas
out; Lady Bullivant led the horses down to the stream; Mogadishu
and the Ndorobo collected firewood; Desmond sat in the shade

and directed. Before long the camp began to take shape. It was oval in construction, horses and blacks one end, Europeans the other. The firewood was heaped in the middle, close to the Landrover.

'Right,' said Desmond, when all was ready. 'I suppose we'd better find out what there is to eat.'

He investigated the contents of the emergency haversack – two cans of baked beans and a tin opener.

'Typical,' he groaned. 'Absolutely bloody typical. Those boys. They've eaten everything.'

This was not a crisis to be taken lightly. Lady Bullivant responded with the spirit of Dunkirk. 'We still have the rifle,' she pointed out. She retrieved it from the Landrover. 'Here, Martin. Go and shoot something for supper.'

Six months ago her words would have filled Martin with terror. Not any more. He took the weapon without a word and checked it over. It was a Rigby, the same one that Desmond had thrust into his hands on his first day in Africa. Only now Martin knew how to use it. He had learned on the shooting range.

There was a herd of impala a mile back, grazing peacefully upwind. Martin cocked his rifle and went off after them on foot.

'We're counting on you,' Eugene told him.

He moved cautiously, careful not to draw attention to himself, keeping a low profile among the thorn trees and thickets of grass. No sudden movements, nothing to cause alarm. He advanced with the instincts of the hunter, making the best use of what little cover was available. At the end of the dry season foliage was sparse, waiting aridly for the rains to bring resuscitation; it was difficult to avoid being seen. But the impala remained impassive, ducking their heads and browsing without concern. Martin crawled the last hundred yards on his belly, cradling his rifle between his elbows, until he was close enough to make out the black tail markings on the nearest bull. It was a fine creature, three feet at the shoulder, with beautiful backswept horns – just the job to lay at the feet of Lady Bullivant.

Martin wriggled forward another few yards onto a tiny hillock covered in undergrowth. He surveyed the bull covertly through a protective screen of grass. Gently, with no outward sign of movement, he brought up his rifle and eased off the safety catch. He parted the grass and took aim.

Just then a flurry of movement caught his eye, a sudden flash of scarlet and black. The impala saw it too. Across the plain, armed with spears and buffalo shields, fully got up for war, came a hundred Masai warriors.

Martin shrank into the grass. Fascinated – horrified – he watched the war party pass between him and the impala, not more than thirty yards away. They were magnificent specimens, six feet every one, daubed in red ochre, their faces streaked with blue clay and lime. They wore iron war rattles and leggings of colobus monkey fur. Their hair was pulled back from their foreheads and hung almost to their waists in greasy red braids. They carried wooden knobkerries and the short two-edged stabbing sword called *simi*. They moved rhythmically, with a purposeful gait, wild and intangible as serval cats. They meant business.

One warrior in particular held Martin's attention. He wore a headdress of black ostrich feathers, a symbol of courage in the tribe, indicating that he had performed some brave deed in the past. Seizing a lion by the tail perhaps, or slaying a dozen enemies in battle. The headdress made him look taller than his contemporaries, more powerfully built. He was a splendid savage, obviously a leader, the embodiment of all that was noble about the Masai, carrying himself with the arrogance of one whose not so distant ancestors had put whole caravans to the sword. He wore a chain of beads around his neck, an elaborate array of ornaments in each ear. The red combat kirtle at his waist revealed a hard, flat stomach and legs decorated from thigh to ankle with intricate designs of clay. He was a fighting man, not an ounce of fat on him, dressed in the bare minimum of clothing, dressed to kill.

He also wore spectacles and tennis shoes, a sight that Martin found vaguely disturbing. Tennis and the Masai, as cultural bedfellows, seemed mutually exclusive somehow, like Rigoletto and rugby league.

The warriors had not seen Martin. Looking neither right nor left, they swept on towards a wooden stockade in a fold of ground close to the Nairobi-Naivasha road. At the entrance to the stockade stood several minibus-loads of tourists, weighed down with cameras and zoom lenses. They had driven from Nairobi for a display of traditional Masai dancing. They were waiting for it to begin.

Wordlessly the warriors marched into the arena and took up their positions. They paid no attention to the audience, but rattled their spears against their shields and launched at once into the first dance of the afternoon. It was a lion dance, Eugene's dance, a regular spectacle at the compound seven days a week. From where he lay Martin could see little of it, save heads bobbing distantly above the walls of the stockade and shoulders trembling at the apex of each warrior's leap to give the impression of more height. But the noise of shuffling feet carried clearly across the bush, like a shunting railway engine. The warriors were dancing with a will, not from enthusiasm for any such activity in the heat of the day, but because tourists were known to be generous with tips after a good performance and the warriors needed money. They were saving for a communal TV.

None of this made any impression on the impala. The Masai seldom hunt wild animals, so there was no danger to the herd. They continued to graze unconcernedly until Martin's shot dropped the leading bull just above the heart. He fell first to his knees, then to the ground, thrashing his hind legs in the air in the last agonies of life. He was quite dead by the time Martin reached him.

Martin heaved the carcass onto his shoulder, steadying it with his left hand, picking up his rifle with his right. He set off for camp, staggering slightly under the burden. Blood oozed from the body and trickled down his shirt. He was soaked when he arrived.

'Keep your head down,' Lady Bullivant told him. 'You don't want the game scout to see you. Mogadishu, give him a hand.'

'Isn't it legal to shoot impala?'

'Certainly not. You're poaching.'

Mogadishu shared the weight. He was disappointed that the

impala was dead. It gave him no chance to slit its throat, as custom demanded.

'*Mzuri tu*,' approved the Ndorobo. He produced a bush knife. 'We cut him up?'

'Sooner the better,' said Desmond.

The Ndorobo went to work. He turned the body over and sliced expertly into the soft skin of the underbelly. The skin peeled off easily, releasing a coil of entrails which fell steaming into the dust.

'You ought to do that with a flint head,' Eugene advised. 'Like they did in the Stone Age.'

'Is okay, bwana. I have a knife.'

Laying open the ribs, the Ndorobo removed a pile of offal and scooped up the contents of the stomach. He cut out the liver with a flourish and offered it to Lady Bullivant.

'One should always eat liver while it's still warm.' She popped a slice into her mouth. 'It's much more chewy that way.'

Blood ran down the corners of her chin. Mogadishu, who liked his meat cooked, watched with fascination.

'Is good, memsabu? *Mzuri*?'

'Absolutely, Mogadishu. You must try some.'

Grinning, Mogadishu shook his head. He did not care to. He went off instead to put some wood on the fire for supper. He was back again soon with a request.

'Matches, bwana. For the fire.'

'Left mine at home,' said Desmond. 'And my ciggies.'

No one else had any either.

'No problem,' Eugene assured them. 'I've been wanting to do this for a long time. All I need is two pieces of wood, one hard, one soft.'

Two sticks were found. Eugene bored a hole in the soft one and inserted the tip of the other into it at right angles. He rubbed the stick vigorously between the palms of his hands. He rubbed for five minutes, hoping for a wisp of smoke. The tip of the wood grew hot to the touch, but no fire appeared. Eugene was disappointed.

'I guess these must be the wrong kinds of sticks,' he said.

As he spoke, a group of Masai warriors suddenly stepped into camp, the same warriors Martin had seen earlier. They had finished dancing for the tourists and had been on their way home until the Landrover had caught their eye.

'Friends of yours?' Desmond asked in alarm. He stood up hastily, studying their weapons.

'I don't think so.' Eugene peered through his spectacles. 'I don't recognise any of them.'

Nor did the Masai appear to recognise Eugene. They had hurried across the bush in the hope of fleecing another party of tourists. They stayed to watch him wrestling with sticks. Something about his sticks evidently intrigued them.

'I'm not sure we want them all in the *boma*, all at once,' Desmond said. 'They're terrible thieves, you know. They steal anything they can lay their hands on.'

'Better ask them to leave,' said Lady Bullivant.

'You speak Masai,' Desmond told Eugene. There was a hint of panic in his voice. 'Ask them what they want.'

'I don't actually *speak* it.'

'Well make yourself understood. We don't want any trouble. Tell them the *laibon* is a friend of yours.'

'Not actually a *friend*.'

'Let me talk to them,' said Martin.

He spoke through the Ndorobo, who knew enough Masai to pass the time of day.

'*Keserian ingera?*'

'*Keserian ingishu.*'

There followed a dialogue of some two thousand words, most of it on the Masai side. Martin listened politely, looking to the Ndorobo for guidance. Gradually it became clear what the warriors were after.

'They're wondering if we'd let them have those tins of beans when they're empty. They use them to make ornaments for their women.'

'They can have them now,' said Desmond. 'No bloody use to us without matches.'

'They've got matches. They'll lend us some to light the fire.'

The leading warrior, he of the tennis shoes, produced a box from underneath his kilt. He gave it to Eugene. Within minutes the fire was ablaze and the meat roasting. Desmond could not trust himself to speak.

Watched by the Masai, they ate impala steaks and beans with their fingers. When they had finished they made a present of the empty cans to the *moran*, and threw in the tin opener for good measure. The warriors seemed grateful. They spat on their palms and shook hands all round, but made no move to go.

'You don't suppose they want to spend the night here?' asked Lady Bullivant.

It was almost dark now. The cold was beginning to bite. Mogadishu heaped wood on the fire; the others huddled round it. Lady Bullivant had appropriated the only blanket – also the Landrover, in which she was proposing to retire for the night with Nkomo.

Desmond held his hands out to the fire and shivered. 'I could just do with a sleeping bag,' he complained.

'Some of the Masai have brought blankets. Perhaps they'd like to sell them?'

'No use to us, Riddle. Full of lice.'

It grew colder.

'We could always smoke them over the fire. To get rid of the bugs.'

'I suppose nobody's got any money?'

Nobody had. Eugene felt in his back pocket and shook his head. 'All I've got is an American Express card.'

The transaction was effected at once. Five blankets changed hands, one for each member of the party. The price was extortionate.

'Supply and demand,' said Desmond.

It was a good evening's work for the Masai. They were well satisfied with their takings. Seeing that there was nothing more to be gained, they picked up their spears and took their leave. One or two tried to sell Desmond a buffalo shield on the way out, but were angrily waved away. The Masai laughed. Led by Tennis Shoes, they set off cheerfully for home, vanishing into the darkness as suddenly as they had come. Long after they had disappeared, they could still be heard across the plain, singing imaginatively about the events of the day.

'Noisy bastards,' said Desmond. He pulled his newly acquired blanket around him and wrinkled his nose. 'Phoof, I think I'm going to throw up.'

'Maybe we'll all get smallpox,' said Eugene.

They settled down to sleep. Lady Bullivant occupied the Land-rover and was already snoring loudly. Mogadishu and the Ndorobo lay down among the horses with their spears easily to hand. Somewhere not far away a hyena could be heard hunting for food. Somewhere too Smith-Baggot was presumably settling down to a lonely vigil. The horses whinnied. Martin joined Eugene and Desmond by the fire and selected a large stone for a pillow. It was amazing how comfortable a stone could be in adversity. Martin lay on his back and looked at the Southern Cross. He could not remember when he had had such an exciting day.

7

He was the only one awake when dawn came. The others, having stayed up half the night alternately scratching themselves and trying to sleep without a blanket, were slumped around the fire in attitudes of exhaustion. Martin had the world to himself. He rose quietly, savouring the splendour of the new day. It was going to be another fine one, almost his last in Africa, certainly his last on the open veld. He would have to begin packing when he returned to Haggard Hall.

As soon as it was fully light he borrowed the spade from the back of the Landrover, taking care not to disturb Lady Bullivant, and tiptoed into the bush on an errand of a personal nature. There was a hollow baobob tree not far from the camp, an imposing sight, large enough inside to accommodate four men – the perfect place for the business Martin had in mind.

Looking round again, he established that he was alone and slipped through the hollow opening. A proper British reticence had led him to the privacy of the baobob in preference to the surrounding plain. It was like a little room inside, light and airy, with a flat earthen floor. He dug a hole in the centre and lowered his trousers. Moments of intense concentration followed. Then he covered the place with tissue paper and turned to go.

He was no longer alone. Yesterday's Masai waited reproachfully outside. One of them wore a tin opener in his ear.

'A prayer tree,' Eugene explained later. 'I should have warned you. That's where the *moran* like to say their prayers.'

The recovery truck arrived at mid-morning. The Padre, sitting in the cab, brought irritating news. Smith-Baggot had given himself up. He had returned to Haggard Hall the previous day, starved into surrender, and had eaten a hearty meal before spending the night comfortably in his own bed. He was sorry for all the aggravation he had caused.

'When I get my hands on him. . . .' said Desmond.

8

And indeed Desmond gave him a thrashing when they got back to school – but Smith-Baggot took it in good part because he didn't care any more. He had changed since they had last seen him. A load had slipped from his shoulders in the past twenty-four hours, a burden of intolerable weight. He was leaving; finished with Haggard Hall. No one could touch him now. He was free.

'You'll like Canterbury,' the Padre told him. 'I was there just after the war.'

Others were less convinced. Smith-Baggot's father in particular. He flew over to discuss this new development with Desmond.

'You don't think we should keep him on another term and try for Charterhouse?'

'Definitely not.'

'Oh well,' said Mr Smith-Baggot, and flew home again.

Nor were the Smith-Baggots willing to travel to England with their son to see his new school. The streets of London were no place for a European, from what they had heard. They referred him instead to an aunt he had never met in Wiltshire. She would collect him from Victoria Station and stand in loco parentis for the length of his stay. Since Martin was leaving too, it was agreed that the two of them should travel to London together.

On the day of their departure, all the staff came out to see them off.

'A safe journey,' Desmond told Martin. 'You're booked on the evening flight. You'll be in London by breakfast tomorrow.'

'I hope I've packed everything.'

'We'll send it on. Mind out with those horns though. Don't let customs see them.'

The horns from Martin's impala had been mounted on a shield for illicit export. They were a trophy, a memento of his time in Africa. He had already mapped out a place for them on his bedroom wall, where his O levels used to hang.

'A decent span.' Desmond measured the width from tip to tip. 'Between you and me, Riddle, I never would have thought it possible when you first arrived out here. Never would. You've come on a lot these last few months.'

'Martin's done very well,' said the Padre.

Mrs Fist slipped her arm through his and gave him a squeeze. 'It's been lovely having you. Give my regards to London. I might end up there myself one of these days.'

Smith-Baggot heaved his suitcase into the car. He had packed his gun and bush knife for the trip to England. Also an elephant hair bracelet, a Kikuyu witch doctor's charm, the hide of a Thomson's gazelle. Also a list of clothing necessary for the summer term at his public school: one black waistcoat, two black jackets, two pairs striped trousers, nine wing collars.

Wing collars?

'You must learn to tie a tie,' Desmond told him. 'Mr Riddle will show you.' He extended a hand. 'Well goodbye, then, Smith-Baggot. All's well that ends well. I'm sorry about Eton, but I dare say it's for the best. Their loss will be Canterbury's gain.'

'Goodbye, sir. Thank you for all you've done for me.'

'You'll find England a strange place to begin with. Not at all suitable for white settlement. Take my advice and play a straight bat for a while, till you know the form.'

'I will, sir.'

'Keep an eye on him,' Desmond advised Martin. 'Don't let him off the plane by himself. We had a boy once, all on his own, never been to England before. Plane made an unscheduled stop at Nice because of headwinds. They had hell's own trouble getting him back on again. He was convinced he'd arrived.'

Martin slipped behind the wheel. The car was due back at the hire company that afternoon. Giving his horns to Smith-Baggot, he groped around the steering column for the ignition. Eugene appeared at the side window and knocked on the glass.

'Have a nice life. I'm off to LA next week to see about my series. I'll send you a postcard.'

'I hope it goes well.'

Martin found the ignition. Now that he was going, he was anxious to be off. The car lurched forward, followed by a chorus of goodbyes around the curve of the drive and on towards the gate. Smith-Baggot leaned out of the window and gave the semblance of a wave. Martin tooted the horn, accidentally. Nkomo made to give chase, but was swiftly called to heel by Lady Bullivant.

'Stupid dog,' said Desmond. 'What was that from Smith-Baggot?'

'I rather think it was two fingers, headmaster.'

'After all we've done for him.'

They lingered to watch the car out of sight. In imagination, for the briefest of moments, they went with it. To Nairobi first, then soaring above the earth, winging across oceans. Somebody leaving always made them think of their own lives, of other people they had known and other places, careers that might have been. Desmond in Australia, the Padre a colonial bishop; the girl Desmond had met on board ship, the offer the Padre had had of a job on *Bird World*. Time past, opportunities missed. An Arab sheikh for Mrs Fist, an India still imperial for Lady Bullivant. The spool of life rewound and played again, differently.

'Geometry, Padre. You'll have to take it on again. We'll need somebody for next term.'

'I can't teach geometry, headmaster.'

As they lingered, a tiny figure came into view where the car had been, hobbling forlornly up the drive towards the school. The Padre adjusted his spectacles. From a distance it looked to be a bird of some kind, bereft of flying feathers, pecked almost to death by a succession of hawks. A bird returning after innumerable adventures to claim his bride, fearful of what might have happened in his absence. Hurrying home as fast as his legs would carry him, hampered only by the message around his ankle: '*St Brendan's 50 all out. Fife-Nugent 6 for 23.*'

9

They were over the English Channel, on course for Gatwick, before it occurred to Martin that he had spent the best part of a year in Kenya without ever seeing an elephant in the wild. He had not even come close.

'You should have tried our place,' Smith-Baggot told him. 'We always get them in the rains.'

Nor, now he thought about it, had he seen a lion or a rhino, unless he counted the droppings scuffed across his path that first day in the Aberdares.

'Some other time,' he said.

It was grey when they came in to land, so grey that all the runway lights were on in broad daylight. Greyer still on the train to London, for the windows had not been washed in months and were crusted with grime. The floor crackled underfoot with crisp packets and old chocolate wrappings. But Smith-Baggot did not notice. He had made the first of many intriguing discoveries about England.

'They have *whites* working on the railway.'

'Whites do all that kind of thing here.'

'Bus drivers too.' Smith-Baggot was disconcerted. 'It doesn't seem right somehow.'

The train passed a row of houses, grimly pebbledashed, each with its own garden and line of washing.

'There isn't much bush here, is there?'

'No.'

'Are those houses two or one?'

'Two. They're called semi-detached. Lots of people live in them.'

Including, although Martin didn't mention it, everyone he knew at Purley Way.

'Can't be much fun. They're all so close together. And look at their *shambas*. You couldn't grow anything on those *shambas*.'

'You don't grow your food here. You buy it from the shops.'

'We wouldn't let our servants live on *shambas* like that.'

Suddenly everything went black. 'Golly!' said Smith-Baggot. 'What's happened?'

'We're in a tunnel.'

'I've never been in a tunnel before.'

'You'll have to get used to the dark, if you're going to live in England.'

Martin put his head out of the window as they pulled in to Victoria. Their carriage was at the end furthest from the barrier, but close enough for him to make out his mother behind the ticket collector's elbow. Also Dad and Gran.

He pulled his head in again. A wave of shame overcame him. He did not want his mother to catch sight of him just yet. He knew exactly what would happen if she did. She would wave frantically and start calling out his name. She would humiliate him in front of Smith-Baggot. Suddenly it was imperative to keep the two of them apart.

He looked round for a means of escape. There was a luggage trolley on the opposite platform; beyond it a tunnel leading to another part of the station. Martin grabbed the trolley. 'We'll go that way,' he decided.

They emerged five minutes later in front of the station, observing the ticket barrier from behind a pile of suitcases. The barrier was deserted now except for the Riddles and a tall, perplexed woman in a headscarf.

'Is that your aunt?'

'I think so.' Smith-Baggot knew her only from photographs.

It was his aunt. Before Martin could stop him, Smith-Baggot went over to introduce himself. They talked. Her head came up, she looked towards the luggage. She saw Martin creeping furtively towards the exit. So did the Riddles.

'You've filled out, Martin! Hasn't he filled out, Dad? And so brown! I hardly recognised you.' Mrs Riddle gave him a hug. 'I hardly did.'

'Like an Indian,' said Dad.

'You didn't write very often. Why didn't you write? You were awfully naughty. You could have sent us a postcard, at least. I wanted to send a telegram to the headmaster to see if anything was wrong, but Dad said not to.'

'The post was pretty bad. Elephants on the line.'

'And leopards. What happened to that leopard?' Mrs Riddle was vague about the details. 'The one that ate the little boy.'

'It's a long story.'

'You must tell us all about it. We'll have a good talk when we get in. We've got steak and prawn cocktail for supper, specially for you. Mrs Simmonds' nephew is coming round afterwards to talk about Nigeria. Do you want to invite your friend? He looks half-starved, poor little mite.'

'Don't worry about Smith-Baggot.'

'And those horns, Martin! You're never going to tell me you killed that all by yourself?'

'I did what had to be done. I was up a volcano at the time. The volcano Ayesha ruled, the heroine of *She*.'

'That must have been nice, dear.'

'There was a programme about it on TV,' said Dad. 'Wild life in Kenya. We all thought of you. We were hoping you might be in it.'

'I'm afraid not.'

'Anyway, Martin. It *is* nice to have you home again.'

173

10

Martin packed his own case for his return to the Regular Commissions Board. His mother fussed around the edges, but he contrived to keep her out of the way until he had filled it to his own satisfaction. Not until he had closed the lid did she have her say.

'You haven't packed your anorak, Martin.'

'No.'

'What will you do if it's cold?'

'Freeze, probably.'

'He's changed,' she complained to her husband. 'He's been a different person since he came back from Africa. I'm not sure I know what to make of him any more.'

'The army will sort him out,' said Dad.

Martin was in Yellow Group this time, number Twenty-three. The others in the group were much as before: a couple of public schoolboys, a couple from grammar school, a staff sergeant who knew about computers, a hard nosed ranker who had seen action in the Falklands. Except for the servicemen, they were little more than boys – most, indeed, still at school. None of them had been to Kenya.

The procedure was the same as before too. It began with the corporal's documentation.

'Name?'

'Riddle.'

'Age last birthday?'

'Twenty-two.'

'Education?'

'There's my O level certificate, there are my A levels, there's my degree. You've got them all in front of you.'

174

'All right, mate. Only doing my job.'

Intelligence tests, the assault course, the discussion group. Martin spoke animatedly, without twiddling his cuffs, about fox hunting and the EEC. He was in favour of both. He argued his case with logic, coherence, lucidity. He was short, sharp and straight to the point.

His lecturette was good too. Every candidate had to speak for five minutes on a subject of their own choosing. Martin's was impala hunting.

'The thing to do when you're hunting impala,' he informed the other candidates, 'is to make optimum use of ground cover. You must never let the impala know you're there. Once they know you're there, pffft, they're gone! Get downwind of them, get on your hands and knees, go for a good clean kill, make sure you've got the right gun for the job. I always use a .270 myself. Then skin them while they're still warm.'

'Keen as mustard, that young man.' The brigadier was impressed. 'Lots of ginger. Haven't we seen him before?'

'We have, sir. You said he was wet.'

'I hardly think I said *that*.'

The planning project, the command task. Martin distinguished himself in both. The planning project was an earthquake job in the jungle, casualties in one direction, important archaeological discoveries in the other. Martin divided his resources with skill. There were not enough llamas to go round, but he made the best use of what was available. He saved all the casualties, most of the artefacts as well.

He knew what to expect from the command task. A heavy weight, a choice of poles, a selection of unreliable ropes. Martin sized up the problem and explained his solution to the others. His voice, throughout, was deeper than it had been before.

'Listen in,' he told them. 'Those are shark-infested waters. Don't waste time, don't hang about. Move when I say move, jump when I say jump. Let's go.'

The candidates went. They jumped when Martin said jump, moved when he told them to move, and arrived breathless at the finishing line with two minutes to spare.

'Well done, Yellow Group,' said the brigadier.

He called Martin to his office for an interview. Martin came, placed his hands on his knees and faced him squarely across the desk.

'I understand you want to join the Education Corps?'

'Not really. I did for a while, but I've been thinking about it and I reckon I might try for the infantry instead. A good line regiment perhaps. The Green Jackets.'

'You want to serve up the sharp end?'

'Yes I do. Education's all very well in its way, but it's not what the army's all about.'

The brigadier agreed. He consulted his file. 'Tell me about Africa. Your time in the bush. How did you get on?'

How had he got on? Martin thought of everything he had seen, everything he had done since he had last been at the Regular Commissions Board. He thought of Lady Bullivant as he would always remember her, hunting little boys on horseback, poisoning the corpses of the servants' children, assaulting leopards with a red hot poker; of how he himself had tracked a human quarry through the jungle and looked a buffalo in the eye; how he had camped on safari in Masai country, spied on a war party in full fig, poached the wild life, had a crap in a sacred prayer tree. He thought of how he had incited a homicidal spearman to burn down a perfectly innocent Catholic mission; had bribed a trio of judges, albeit by proxy; had climbed Ayesha's volcano and walked the plains of *King Solomon's Mines*. All these things he thought of before he spoke.

'I got on all right.'

'And you think you could command a platoon of ex-borstal boys in the Crumlin Road?'

Martin thought of Fife-Nugent's tarantula, of Nightshade's soldier ants, of the Ndorobo cutting off gobs of liver with his knife.

'I'm sure I could,' he said.

The army evidently agreed. When Martin returned to Purley Way, a letter was already waiting for him on the sideboard. It contained his joining instructions for Sandhurst.

'I always knew you'd get in,' said Mrs Riddle.